mustsees
Alaska

Aurora over Eagle River © Roy Neese/Visit Anchorage

D1173314

mustsees **Alaska**

Editorial Director	Cynthia Clayton Ochterbeck
Editor	Gwen Cannon
Writer	Eric Lucas
Production Manager	Natasha George
Cartography	Peter Wrenn
Photo Researcher	Nicole D. Jordan
Layout	Nicole D. Jordan
Interior Design	Chris Bell, cbdesign, Natasha George
Cover Design	Chris Bell, cbdesign, Natasha George

Contact Us

Michelin Travel and Lifestyle North America
One Parkway South
Greenville, SC 29615, USA
travel.lifestyle@michelin.com

Michelin Travel Partner
Hannay House
39 Clarendon Road
Watford, Herts WD17 1JA, UK
www.ViaMichelin.com
travelpubsales@uk.michelin.com

Special Sales

For information regarding bulk sales, customized editions and premium sales, please contact us at:
travel.lifestyle@michelin.com

Michelin Travel Partner

Société par actions simplifiées au capital de 11 288 880 EUR
27 cours de l'Ile Seguin - 92100 Boulogne Billancourt (France)
R.C.S. Nanterre 433 677 721

© Michelin Travel Partner
ISBN 978-2-067216-17-4
Printed: December 2016
Printed and bound in Italy

Welcome to Alaska

© Lark Carlson Brown/Bigstockphoto.com

Introduction

Dog sledding/©Leslie Forsberg/Michelin

p 14

© Leslie Forsberg/Michelin

p 55

Must Do

© Jacob W. Frank/NPS (CC-by-2.0)

© Leslie Forsberg/Michelin

Gates of the Arctic/©Leslie Forsberg/Michelin

TABLE OF CONTENTS

★★★ ATTRACTIONS

Unmissable historic, cultural and natural sights

Alaska SeaLife Center   p 78

©Alaska SeaLife Center Staff

Alaska Native Heritage Center   p 66

© Ashley Johnston/Visit Anchorage

Kodiak National Wildlife Refuge   p 113, 115

©Dave Menke/U.S. Fish and Wildlife Service

MUST KNOW

©Leslie Forsberg/Michelin

Mendenhall Glacier p 46

© Ken Graham Photography/Anchorage Museum

Anchorage Museum p 66

© Tim Rains/NPS (CC-by-2.0)

Denali National Park p 98, 101

★★★ ATTRACTIONS

Unmissable historic, cultural and natural sights

For some 90 years people have used Michelin stars to take the guesswork out of travel. Our star-rating system helps you make the best decision on where to go, what to do, and what to see.

★★★	Unmissable	★	Worth a detour
★★	Worth a trip	No star	Recommended

MUST KNOW

ACTIVITIES

Unmissable activities, entertainment, restaurants and hotels

Alaska's glorious landscapes and awesome animals add a sense of drama to human activities there. We recommend every activity in this guide, but the Michelin Man logo highlights our top picks.

Outings

Admire Native art *pp 73, 87*
Bike the coast *p 70*
Cruise the Panhandle *p 126*
Fish for salmon *p 78*
Flightsee by helicopter *p 125*
Fly in a floatplane *p 115*
Gawk at glaciers *p 11*
Hike beneath Denali *p 103*
Linger at a lagoon *p 72*
Pan for gold *p 75*
Relive history *p 53, 55, 89, 91*
Ride a tram *pp 45, 74*
Take a train *p 53*
Watch a dogsled race *pp 83, 119*
View wildlife *p 102*

Hotels

Alaska Backpackers Inn *p 144*
A Channel View B&B *p 150*
Chena Hot Springs cabins *p 91*
Gustavus Inn *p 149*
Hotel Alyeska *p 145*
Hotel Captain Cook *p 145*
Pearson's Pond Luxury Inn *p 149*
Pike's Waterfront Lodge *p 147*
Seward Windsong Lodge *p 150*
Talkeetna Alaskan Lodge *p 151*

Nightlife

Cape Fox Dancers *p 60*
Frantic Follies *p 97*
Gathering Place *p 67*
Jazz *p 20*
Native dance at Alaska State Fair *p 21*
New Archangel Dancers *p 58*
Sheet'ka Kwaan Naa Kahidi Native Dancers *p 58*

Relax

Admire the aurora borealis *p 88*
Bite a bison burger *p 148*
Browse for books *p 73*
Dawdle in a deckchair *p 122*
Putter on a porch *pp 100, 149*
Soak in a hot spring *p 91*
Tour totems *pp 60, 61*
Zone out at the zoo *p 71*

Restaurants

Chena's Alaskan Grill *p 148*
Kincaid Grill *p 136*
Ludvig's Bistro *p 141*
Old Powerhouse *p 141*
Orso *p 136*
Pumphouse *p 139*
The Rookery *p 140*
Seven Glaciers Restaurant *p 137*
Snow City Café *p 135*

Shopping

Fur coats David Green Master Furrier *p 73*
Native art *pp 46, 73*
Indigenous Crafts *p 73*
Souvenirs *p 59*
T-shirts *p 101*

Side Trips

Gold Dredge 8 *p 93*
Kluane National Park *p 96*
Shore excursions *p 125*
Whitehorse *p 97*

Sports

Biking *p 70*
Hiking *pp 53, 100*
Golfing *pp 72, 84*
Ice climbing *p 15*
Ice skating *p 72*
Kayaking *pp 11, 153*
Skiing *p 14, 74*

STAR ATTRACTIONS

IDEAS AND TOURS

Throughout this thematic guide you will find inspiration for many different ways to experience Alaska. The following is a selection of places and activities from the guide to help start you off. The sights in bold are found in the index.

CRUISING

Alaska and cruises go together like bread and butter. Aside from the famous **Inside Passage★★** among the coastal islands to ports of call like Skagway, Juneau and Sitka in SE Alaska *(see Cruising Alaska)*, **Alaska Marine Highway** serves as the state's principal water taxi: a number of ocean passages can be booked for marine crossings *(see Practical Information)*, many of them simply to get from point A to B. In Fairbanks, **Riverboat Discovery★** *(late May–late Sept)* on the Chena River is a pleasant half-day float, with a stop at a replica Athabaskan fish camp village. Farther afield, in Canada's neighboring Yukon Territory, a 2hr cruise on the mighty Yukon River passes through the steep walls of **Miles Canyon★**. Day cruises offered by Kenai Fjords Tours *(Mar–Oct)* depart from Seward for **Kenai Fjords National Park★★** to watch whales and sea lions and visit **tidewater glaciers**; two of the boats are high-speed catamarans, and some sailings have National Park Service

What's 'inside' the Inside Passage?

Used by mariners for eons to avoid the Gulf of Alaska's dangerous seas, the famous sheltered **shipping lane** between Seattle and Alaska follows channels "inside" coastal islands that fend off North Pacific swells. For more than 100 years, the route has been used by cruise ships; it brings passengers past lush islands, through calm, emerald-waters, beneath towering snowy mountains and near narrrow fjords with waterfalls plunging from the heights.

In essence, every cruise that sails from Seattle to Alaska and back (thus traversing the coast of British Columbia as well) travels a route that could be called the Inside Passage, including itineraries sailed by the biggest cruise ships, in the 3,000-passenger class, that could safely sail "outside" on open ocean. To save time, many ships depart Seattle or Vancouver and end their voyages by passing along the outer coast of Vancouver Island. Once they reach Alaskan waters, they head "inside" to access Ketchikan, Juneau, Glacier Bay and other coastal destinations. When these boats get back to the 49th parallel, they dock for a half-day or so in Victoria, British Columbia, to satisfy an obscure legal requirement that's one of the greatest examples of the law of unintended consequences: the Jones Act. Adopted in the US in the late 19C, it requires that cruise ships sailing only between US ports must be built in the US. Intended to save the US shipbuilding industry, the law has accomplished nothing of the sort. Instead, virtually all major cruise ships that are built in Europe or Asia stop in a foreign port, thus skirting the law. Victoria is such a port. When your ship berths in that city, take advantage of the chance to stroll into a delightful small city.

Seeing Alaska by helicopter

© Travel Juneau

naturalists onboard. Stan Stephens Cruises in Valdez make their way (*mid-May–mid-Sept*) through **Prince William Sound**★★ to the fjord that holds the Columbia Glacier. Passengers on the 8hr cruise are certain to see otters, sea lions and whales. **Bristol Bay**, off the Alaska Peninsula, is a sparsely settled basin whose lakes and rivers host the world's largest single **salmon fishery**. Visitors can arrange to spend a day on a commercial fishing boat and tour a processing plant or both.

GLACIER GAZING

Glaciers and Alaska are synonymous. The state has an estimated 10,000 of them. Perhaps the most famous is the 12mi river of ice known as the **Mendenhall Glacier**★★★, which flows down from the 1,500sq-mi Juneau Icefield in the coastal mountains above. **Glacier treks**★★ to it with experienced guides are popular with Juneau visitors. (Tip: Avoid busloads of tourists by visiting Mendenhall Glacier before 10am.) If you want to witness glaciers calve (shed blocks into the water), **Glacier Bay National Park**★★ is the place to see it. Visitors board boats for a day-long cruise through

the long, mountain-ringed fjord. On foot, the most easily reached glacier is **Exit Glacier**★★, outside Seward. A short hike *(1.4mi)* through cottonwood forest leads visitors to viewpoints beside the glacier. Dayboat cruises in Prince William Sound (Valdez and Whittier) and Resurrection Bay (Seward) bring passengers near massive tidewater glaciers. At Portage, near Anchorage, boating across the terminal lake is the only way to view the namesake **Portage Glacier**★, which has retreated far up its valley. Today, visitors must paddle themselves across the lake to view the glacier, or avail themselves of boat tours *(mid-May-mid-Sept)*. North of Anchorage, in the Matanuska Valley, **Matanuska Glacier** is one glacier that visitors can fairly easily drive near or walk onto; a hiking trail provides great views of its terminus, which is on private property and is accessible only by guide service at the glacier's foot.

FISHING AND KAYAKING

Fishing is a big sport in Alaska, both angling in rivers and aboard ocean charters. **Salmon fishing** draws thousands of anglers to the

11

Portage Glacier

1944, but hopeful gold-seekers can pan in the creek below. At **Gold Dredge 8★**, near Fairbanks, visitors learn how these massive machines extracted ore from streambeds—and visitors who elect to pan for gold actually find some.

🥾 HIKING

Anchorage's famed 10mi urban **Tony Knowles Coastal Trail★★** edges Cook Inlet's shoreline, revealing, per chance, an occasional moose but plenty of birdlife. In south Anchorage, the short (*1.5mi*) but steep **Flattop Mountain Trail** in **Chugach State Park★★** offers a spectacular viewpoint. In the late 19C, gold-rushers by the hundreds struggled up the legendary **Chilkoot Trail** out of Skagway. Adventurers can still hike the trail today—an arduous, three-day journey; national park permits are required and fees up to $50 are charged, depending on the length you hike. **Tongass National Forest**'s rich rain forests make for rewarding rambles, and in **Denali National Park★★★** hikes across subarctic tundra are possible. Just southwest of downtown Anchorage, hiking trails encircle **Westchester Lagoon★**, a wetland preserve anchoring the shoreline end of the Chester Creek greenbelt trail. Ospreys, eagles, ducks, loons and geese are common summer sights. Girdwood's popular Alyeska Ski Resort has hiking trails that lead into nearby temperate rain forest—perhaps the northernmost in North America. Within **Kenai Fjords National Park★★**, the **Harding Icefield Trail★** is a strenuous (*4.1mi*) uphill day-hike to viewpoints overlooking the vast

town of Seward in July and August, when several species of Pacific salmon, including chinook, coho and sockeye, are running in local rivers. Charter excursions generally run $200-$400 a day, and include all costs such as licensing, gear, and fish packing. Summer salmon runs in **Prince William Sound★★** also draw fishing enthusiasts. **Westchester Lagoon★**, southwest of Anchorage, makes a pleasant paddle amid a wetland busy with waterfowl. Kayak rentals are available at Fairbanks' **Pioneer Park** to float the **Chena River**, a delightful two-hour excursion.

⛏ GOLD MINING

Discoveries of gold are inextricably etched into Alaska's colorful history. Modern-day fortune-seekers can stake out a "claim" and try their luck—usually for a nominal fee—at several mines. **Crow Creek Mine** is a historic (1896) gold-mining operation near Girdwood; visitors can pan for gold there today. Juneau's **Last Chance Mining Museum** occupies old mine buildings decommissioned in icefield. In the vicinity of Wrangell-St. Elias National Park, **Kennecott Mines National Historic Landmark**★★ is the trailhead for **Root Glacier Trail**★, an easy 2mi hike along the valley edge to the nearest glacier, descending from Regal Mountain.

NATIVE CULTURE

Learn about Alaska's major indigenous groups, from the Inupiaq to the Alutiiq at **Alaska Native Heritage Center**★★★ in Anchorage. Exhibits range from historic baskets to modern art. Native dance, chant, song and story-telling are performed on the grounds, and six life-size reconstructed traditional dwellings can be seen. The center is a good place to buy real Native art as is the gift shop at the **Alaska Native Medical Center** in Anchorage. In Juneau the **Alaska State Museum**★★★ exhibits a collection of Native arts and artifacts that include a massive 32ft walrus-skin kayak. At **Saxman Village**★ in Ketchikan, visitors can watch traditional dance, chant and song performed in a huge longhouse.

TRAMS AND TRAINS

At Alyeska Resort near Girdwood, the **Alyeska Tram**★★ rises 2,025ft up a precipitous slope at the resort, taking visitors to a knob at 2,334ft elevation for spectacular views of **Turnagain Arm**, the Kenai Peninsula and the Chugach Mountains. In Juneau, the ride on the **Mount Roberts Tram**★★ rises to 1,745ft along a steep slope on its namesake mountain, providing the best overlook of the city and the surrounding peaks. The narrow gauge **White Pass & Yukon Route Railway**★★ (*early May- late Sept*) follows a scenic (and sometimes harrowing) route up its namesake pass. Most Skagway visitors hop aboard a morning train of restored period railcars for a half-day excursion to the pass summit, along which the train climbs 3,000ft in 20mi.

The **Alaska Railroad** is not only one of the very best ways to travel between Seward, Anchorage, Denali National Park and Fairbanks, its route is scenic virtually the entire way; high-dome observation cars offer passengers all the views one could ask. Journeys on the train are memorable

Alaska State Museum's gallery of Yup'ik and Inupiaq Native culture, with 34ft umiak

© Lara Swimmer/Alaska State Museum

scenic odysseys—several of the best spots to view Denali, when the weather is clear, are along the railroad line approaching Talkeetna. For a much shorter excursion, board the Iron Horse Train for a narrow-gauge circuit circling Fairbanks' **Pioneer Park★**.

WILDLIFE VIEWING

Alaska is a paradise for spotting wildlife. Sitka black-tailed deer can be seen in the Panhandle's rain forest. Musk-ox graze the tundra of Nome, and caribou roam **Denali National Park★★★**. Indeed, Denali visitors often see bears, moose, Dall sheep and even wolves, as well. In Resurrection Bay, bordering **Kenai Fjords National Park★★**, orcas, humpback whales, sea otters, puffins and Dall's porpoises are usually visible in the water, and mountain goats on the steep cliffs overlooking the bay. **Potter Marsh Bird Sanctuary★**, south of Anchorage, affords glimpses of trumpeter swans, Arctic terns, various ducks, and raptors such as the northern harrier. Along the **Alaska Highway★★**, Dall sheep can usually be seen in the vicinity of Sheep Mountain. Grizzly (brown) bears, moose and eagles visit the Chilkat River in Haines. **Kodiak National Wildlife Refuge★★★** encompasses nearly 3,000sq mi to protect the rugged, undeveloped landscape in which 3,000 **Kodiak bears** roam. Visiting the refuge is possible only by floatplane or boat, however. In **Katmai National Park★★** brown bears fish for salmon atop **Brooks Falls★★**, a 10ft cataract marking the spot that Brooks Lake drains into Naknek Lake. Annual salmon runs here draw large numbers of

coastal brown bears to feast on the fish. If you're disappointed in your sightings in the wild, head for Anchorage's **Alaska Zoo★** to see Alaska musk-ox, moose, porcupines, Dall sheep and wolves, among other animals. Seward's **Alaska SeaLife Center★★★**, the only aquarium in Alaska, shelters otters, seals, Steller sea lions and other maritime denizens of the North Pacific.

WINTER ACTIVITIES

The things you can do in winter in Alaska are almost endless: dogsledding in Fairbanks, viewing the Northern Lights while soaking in Chena Hot Springs near Fairbanks, Nordic skiing near Talkeetna, alpine skiing at Alyeska Ski Resort outside Anchorage in Girdwood, ☃ **ice climbing** near the **Matanuska Glacier**—and snowmobiling nearly everywhere. The Kenai peninsula offers wild Alaska at its best: it's famous for wilderness trekking, wildlife watching and winter sports.

Skiing

Alaska has snow—lots of it, for a long time each winter. The key ingredient for ski resorts that the state lacks is people, so there are notable Alpine skiing areas with established seasons and a modicum of visitor facilities (such as rental equipment) only near Anchorage, Juneau and Fairbanks.

♦ **Alyeska Resort** *(907-754-1111; www.alyeskaresort.com)*. This huge area in Girdwood, an hour south of Anchorage, has a tram, a 2,500ft vertical, 1,500 skiable acres, deep snow from November through

April, a huge hotel, and lots of runs and bowls, ranging from advanced to beginner. It's the only area in Alaska that draws travelers from outside the state.

♦ **Eaglecrest Ski Area:** Located on Douglas Island near Juneau, this modest day use area has reliable snow, several chairlifts, lots of good intermediate territory and a friendly atmosphere (*www.skijuneau.com*).

♦ **Birch Hill**: This small area near Fairbanks rises on the grounds of Fort Wainwwright military base; it offers a modest downhill skiing area, as well as cross-country skiing (*ftwainwrightfmwr.com*).

Virtually all Alaska cities and towns have Nordic skiing trail networks in or near them; in Southeast Alaska, where snow doesn't always reach to sea level, skiing is usually found in the mountains nearby. Anchorage, notably, turns its extensive recreation trail network into what is surely the largest Nordic ski facility in the country each winter—literally hundreds of miles are groomed, trails reach into every neighborhood, and winter visitors may easily rent skis (check at REI) and ski almost out the door.

DRIVING TOURS

With far fewer highways than other US states, driving in Alaska is more limited—but the places one can drive to are among the most memorable landscapes and most-sought attractions in North America. Here are suggestions for driving tours:

Alaska Highway★★

10 days; about 2,700mi (one way). May through September.
Though it's no longer the great

Skiing at Alyeska Resort

© Jack Bonney/Visit Anchorage

adventure on unpaved road it once was, this immense journey does take travelers through some of North America's most spectacular landscapes.

For comprehensive detailed information about the highway and the destinations and facilities along it, consult *The Milepost*, an annual guide to traveling this great road; *milepost.com*.

The tour begins in **Seattle,** the sparkling city on Puget Sound. Drive north to **Vancouver**, British Columbia, home of the 2010 Winter Olympics, Stanley Park and the famous UBC Museum of Anthropology. Then head west and north up the Fraser River Valley, passing the **Fraser Canyon** and Hells Gate, on through the **Cariboo** region, rich in cattle and gold rush history, to Prince George. Mile 1 of the Alaska Highway is in **Dawson Creek**, BC; from here, head north through the **Northern Rockies** past such scenic sights as Muncho Lake Provincial Park, making sure to stop at Liard River Hot Springs.

15

Cross into Canada's Yukon Territory to **Whitehorse**★, the small-city capital. An optional detour is north up to **Dawson City** and the heart of Klondike history; otherwise, travel west past **Kluane National Park**★★, part of the world's largest international mountain wilderness preserve. Cross into Alaska near **Tetlin National Wildlife Refuge**, turning south at Tok Junction. Head down past **Wrangell-St. Elias National Park**★★, largest in the US, before turning west toward Anchorage at Glenallen. Pass down the **Matanuska Valley**, along the Chugach Mountains and the vast Matanuska Glacier, before arriving in **Palmer**, heart of Alaska's farming country. Then a few hours south along the upper reaches of Cook Inlet bring you to Alaska's largest city, **Anchorage**★.

On the return (2, 700mi, 10 days, one way), an alternate routing is to pass through Whitehorse and turn south on the **Cassiar Highway** near Watson Lake. This mountain road, still mostly unpaved, is more remote and less crowded than the Alaska Highway; it brings you past the burly **Stikine River**, then down into the **Skeena River Valley**, from where you head back east to Prince George and thence back to Seattle.

Kenai Splendor

3 days; about 515mi.
Best from April to October

This route takes you along scenic Turnagain Arm, and down into the famous Kenai Peninsula's mountains, glaciers and wildlife, winding up in the quaint village of Homer.

From **Anchorage**★, head south on the Seward Highway, passing along the surging tidal waters of **Turnagain Arm**. Stop in the village of **Girdwood**, home of Alyeska Resort and the **Alyeska Tram**; then return to the highway for the drive past Portage and down the heart of the Kenai Peninsula to the port of **Seward**★★, home of the Alaska Sealife Center and **Resurrection Bay**★ boat tours. Then retrace your steps to the Sterling Highway, turning south toward **Kenai**, traveling along the shores of southern Cook Inlet to the picturesque village of **Homer**★. A ferry ride brings you across mountain-ringed Kachemak Bay to **Seldovia**. Next day, retrace your route back to Anchorage.

The "Golden Heart"

7 days; about 880mi.
Not suggested in winter.

This route takes travelers past Denali National Park, home of America's highest peak, thence on to Fairbanks, capital of Interior Alaska and a historic gold rush town; and on around back to Anchorage up the Tanana River Valley and down the scenic Matanuska Valley.

Begin in **Anchorage**★. The **Anchorage Museum**★★★ is one of the best in the country devoted to Native Alaskan art and artifacts. The drive up to Palmer leads you into the scenic Susitna Valley, where **Talkeetna** is a quaint historic town with a great view of 20,320ft Denali on clear days. Its ranger station serves as headquarters for Denali climbers. From here, head north to the "town" of Denali, the entrance to **Denali National Park**★★★, one of America's most famous. Stop here for a day to **tour the park** in special buses whose drivers are also knowledgeable park guides. Then head up through boreal forest to **Fairbanks★**, capital of Alaska's Interior, home of the popular Riverboat Discovery and gold mining history. The **Museum of the North★★★** here has an impressive collection of Alaskan art, both Native and modern. Then go southeast from Fairbanks to **Tok Junction**, returning along **Wrangell-St Elias National Park★★**, America's largest, to Anchorage along the scenic **Matanuska Valley**.

Gold Rush Trails

6 days; about 1,300mi.
June through September only.
This route takes you along the "Top of the World" to the heart of the Klondike, then through the wild and untamed Yukon to Fairbanks. Start in **Fairbanks**, center of the Alaska Interior and home of the Riverboat Discovery and the **Museum of the North★★★**. Head south along the Alaska Highway through Tok Junction, turning north on the **Top of the World Highway**, a scenic and still-wild passage across the mountains bordering Yukon Territory. Descend into **Dawson City**, historic capital of the Klondike Gold Rush in the late 19C, with sights such as the Robert Service Cabin and the Bonanza Creek Mining District. Then head south to **Whitehorse★**, charming small city capital of the Yukon, with attractions such as the **Beringia Interpretive Centre** and the SS Klondike riverboat. Return to Fairbanks along the Alaska Highway, passing **Kluane National Park★★** and **Tetlin National Wildlife Refuge**.

Quick Trips
Stuck for ideas? Try these:

IDEAS AND TOURS

17

CALENDAR OF EVENTS

Listed below is a selection of Alaska's most popular annual events; dates often vary from year to year. For detailed information on these and other festivals, visit the event websites of local tourism offices or Travel Alaska *(www.travelalaska.com).*

January

Anchorage Folk Festival
www.anchoragefolkfestival.org
It may be dark and cold outside in late January, but indoors there's a lot of singing, dancing, hand-clapping and storytelling during this midwinter festival.

February

Yukon Quest
early Feb; *www.yukonquest.com*
Adherents swear the 1,000mi sled dog race between Fairbanks and Whitehorse, Yukon, is tougher than the Iditarod. Festivities greet the start and finish in each city.

Fur Rendezvous
late Feb into early March;
www.furrondy.net
Spread over two weekends and the week between, this Anchorage event is one of the most engaging, imaginative and colorful community festivals in the country.

Festival of Native Arts
late Feb; *fna.community.uaf.edu*
Indigenous peoples from throughout Alaska—and all of North America—throng the University of Alaska Fairbanks for this three-day celebration. Native dance, song, chant, storytelling, crafts and art fill the event hall.

World Ice Art Championships
late Feb through March;
www.icealaska.com
Carvers wielding chainsaws, chisels, brushes and other tools come from around the world to

February: "Fighter" by Junichi Nakamura, Shinichi Sawamura, Dean Murray and Chan Kitburi World Ice Art Championships

© Karen H Clautice/Ice Alaska

MUST KNOW

18

Fur Rendezvous

The isolation and inactivity of Alaska's long winter led early Anchorage leaders to create a family-oriented festival tabbed to the historic pioneer gatherings at which fur trappers congregated to sell their catch, enjoy social activities and indulge in sports. A **fur auction** remains a key part of Fur Rendezvous, which takes place over two weekends and the week in between, each year in late February and early March. Anchorage residents take part in, or observe, serious competitions such as the World Championship Sled Dog Sprint Races, which start and end on downtown streets. More quintessential are the not-so-serious frolics, such as the Outhouse Race (on sleds), the Snowshoe Softball Tournament, and the hugely popular Running of the Reindeer, in which hundreds of human racers sprint along 4th Avenue with, yes, reindeer.

Fairbanks for this competition, which is the premier event of its kind. Their works remain on display for weeks in the festival's new park.

March
Iditarod Trail Sled Dog Race
first half of March; *iditarod.com*

By far the most famous dogsledding competition begins in early March with a ceremonial start in downtown Anchorage, continues with a real start in Willow the next day, and concludes about 9 days and 1,049mi later in Nome. This endurance race across frozen mountains, rivers, forests and tundra follows the route used in 1925 to relay diphtheria serum to Nome from Seward.

May
Kachemak Bay Shorebird Festival
early May; *www.homeralaska.org*

The waters surrounding Homer are home to millions of waterfowl and shorebirds, most migratory, and early May is the period when they throng here in greatest numbers. This community festival celebrates the avian bounty with organized birdwatching programs and interpretive presentations.

Juneau Jazz and Classics
first half of May;

jazzandclassics.org

Top musicians from around the country find their way to the state capital for this two-week performance festival.

Great Alaska Beerfest
mid-May; *seakfair.org/beer-fest*

Visitors throng to Haines to camp out and revel in the city's thriving craft beer and distillery industry.

Kodiak Crab Festival
late May into June;

www.kodiak.org

Both snow and king crab are the focus of this five-day event that includes a parade, carnival, survival suit races and of course, lots of crab comesting.

June
Sitka Summer Music Festival
throughout June;

www.sitkamusicfestival.org

Top-notch chamber music

performers wend their way to Sitka for this month-long event. Performances take place in the city's Centennial Hall.

July
Mount Marathon Race
July 4; *www.seward.com*

Thousands flock to Seward to watch hardy adventurers relive a supposed bar bet from decades ago: can someone run up nearby Mount Marathon to its 3,022ft summit and back in one hour?

Gold Rush Days
late June to early July;
www.traveljuneau.com/events

Juneau re-creates its lively boom days with a weekend festival that consists of mining contests (jack leg drilling, anyone?) one day and logging competitions the next. Salmon, crab and Alaska prawns are on hand for the hungry.

World Eskimo Indian Olympics
mid-July; *www.weio.org*

The famous blanket toss is the culmination of this colorful competition in Fairbanks, which also includes stick pulls, high kicks (one- and two-foot) and seal hops. Dance performances, regalia contests and other traditional activities round out the four-day event.

August
Valdez Silver Salmon Derby
late Jul-early September;
www.valdezfishderbies.com

Silver—coho—salmon start arriving in Prince William Sound in late July, running strong into area rivers through early September. Valdez has various fishing derbies devoted to this bounty: one day is devoted to a women's derby, Fridays offer extra prizes. Anyone can take part.

Ketchikan Blueberry Arts Festival
early August; *ketchikanarts.org*

Juried art shows, band competitions, a slug race and of course, blueberry pie-making and pie-eating contests mark this annual affair.

June: On stage at Harrigan Centennial Hall, Sitka Summer Music Festival

© Christine Davenport/Sitka Summer Music Festival

Whale of a Good Time

Alaska's waters are home to, notably, humpback and gray whales. Both migrate from warm southern waters—mostly Hawaii, in the case of humpbacks, and Mexico for grays—to the biologically rich waters of the Gulf of Alaska to fatten on herring, krill and other food-fish. Their young have been born over the winter and accompany their mothers north. Alaskans have welcomed this annual 2,000mi migration for centuries. The first whales arrive in the Sitka area in **late March**, coinciding with an early spring herring spawn, and work their way northward from there. Both grays and humpbacks head back south starting in **late August**, with stragglers sometimes hanging on until November. Orcas (killer whales) also inhabit Alaska waters.

Alaska State Fair
late August into early September;
www.alaskastatefair.org
Cabbages as big as wagons and turnips the size of pumpkins are the famed attractions at this fair in Palmer, an hour north of Anchorage, which celebrates the thriving diversity of agriculture in the Great Land. Concerts, lumberjack competitions and Native dance performances liven things up.

October
Alaska Day
mid-Oct;
www.alaskadayfestival.org
Though October 18 is the actual state holiday celebrating the transfer of Alaska from Russia to the US, a mid-month, weeklong festival in Sitka includes a formal ball, a parade, community frolics and a full-dress re-enactment of the 1867 handover ceremony.

November
Sitka Whalefest
early Nov;
www.sitkawhalefest.org
Scientists and cetacean enthusiasts from around the world gather in Sitka—just as the last whales are headed south for the winter—to discuss new research findings and conservation measures. Concerts and art shows round out the events.

December
Talkeetna Bachelor Auction
early Dec;
www.bachelorsoftalkeetna.org
Yes, Talkeetna is different—a fact proved every year at the annual evening affair during which ladies bid on a drink and dance with the bachelor of their choice. The auction is preceded by the annual "Wilderness Woman Contest" that was, er, dreamed up by the bachelors to identify ladies whose mettle met the demands of Alaska.

Christmas in Ice
throughout December;
www.christmasinice.org
A month-long ice-carving festival in North Pole, just outside Fairbanks, brings artists from around the country. A children's play area complete with ice slides and an outdoor picnic adds to the fun for youngsters.

PRACTICAL INFORMATION

WHEN TO GO

The diversity of Alaska's geographic regions is extreme—in Southeast Alaska, a **maritime climate** means temperatures are rarely very cold, but copious amounts of precipitation create a temperate rain forest. In south-central Alaska, around Anchorage, **winters** are cold, with temperatures below zero F, but enough warmth arrives in summer that farmers nearby in the Palmer area grow an array of crops. In the Interior, around Fairbanks, **summers** are warm and rainy, while winters are largely dry but at times quite cold—the record low is -66°F. Always have an umbrella. The vast majority of visitors come here between late May and early September, in the belief it's the best time. Whether that's true depends on what you come to see, for Alaska's climate poses conundrums outsiders do not realize.

Late April and May, for instance, often bring the best weather in Southeast Alaska, with the least rain and the most sun, though temperatures remain cool—highs around 60°F. June, July and August usually bring the greatest warmth in Anchorage and Fairbanks; but also may be rainy and cloudy, a great disappointment if intent on seeing the peak of Denali. **September** marks the start of fall, with rain and clouds across Alaska. The annual migration of visitors, largely cruise passengers (1 million a year) begins around May 15, peaks in late June, and proceeds unabated until early September. If you dislike crowds, avoid popular destinations after May 15 and before Labor Day.

Prices climb along with tourist arrivals; the best bargains are in March and April, as well as September and October.

It's best to see the **Northern Lights** in March, when severe winter temperatures moderate, skies are often clear, but days have not lengthened so much that daylight interferes with viewing. *Current weather conditions are online: www.weather.com or www.cnn.com/weather.*

KNOW BEFORE YOU GO
Useful Websites

www.travelalaska.com – Official state tourism website for vacation and travel information.
www.alaska.gov – Official state government website has a visitor section with community profiles.

Average Low/High Temperatures in Alaska

	Jan	Apr	Jul	Oct
Anchorage	9°F/21°F	30°F/42°F	52°F/65°F	30°F/40°F
Utqiagvik (Barrow)	−19°F/−8°F	−10°F/5°F	33°F/45°F	9°F/18°F
Fairbanks	−18°F/0°F	20°F/42°F	52°F/72°F	18°F/32°F
Juneau	20°F/29°F	32°F/48°F	48°F/65°F	38°F/48°F
Kodiak	0°F/12°F	18°F/32°F	49°F/62°F	25°F/35°F

MUST KNOW

Anchorage Visitor Information Center

© Roy Neese/Visit Anchorage

www.dnr.state.ak.us/parks –
Alaska Division of Parks & Outdoor
Recreation.

www.nps.gov/akso – Alaska
Regional Office, National Park
Service.

www.alaskageographic.org –
The partner for the state's national
parks is devoted to education and
conservation.

www.nature.org – Nature
Conservancy owns hundreds of
private land preserves in the West.
The organization sponsors trips
and tours.

**www.academicinfo.net/
amwest.html** – The best source
for comprehensive information on
Western history.

www.snocountry.com and
www.onthesnow.com – The two
key sites to track ski conditions,
updated each morning.

www.weather.com and **www.
cnn.com/weather** – National
weather forecasting websites.

Tourism Offices

The Alaska state tourism office
website (www.travelalaska.com)
provides information on points
of interest, seasonal events and
accommodations, as well as road
and city maps and a free brochure
Alaska Vacation Planner that can be
ordered online. The website lists
contact information for many city
and regional tourism offices

◆ **Alaska Travel Industry
   Association**, 2600 Cordova St.,
   Ste. 201, Anchorage, AK 99503.
   907-274-7579.
   www.travelalaska.com.

Local tourist offices listed below
provide information free of charge
about accommodations, shopping,
entertainment, festivals and
recreation.

◆ **Anchorage**
   524 W. 4th Avenue
   Anchorage, AK 99501-2212
   907-276-4118, 800-478-1255
   www.anchorage.net
◆ **Fairbanks**
   101 Dunkel Street, Ste 111
   Fairbanks, AK 99701
   907-456-5774, 800-327-5774
   www.explorefairbanks.com
◆ **Juneau**
   800 Glacier Avenue, Suite 201
   Juneau, AK 99801
   907-586-2201, 888-581-2201
   www.traveljuneau.com

PRACTICAL INFORMATION

23

◆ **Kodiak**
100 Marine Way at the Ferry
Terminal in Kodiak
907-486-4782, 800-789-4782
www.kodiak.org

International Visitors

US Embassies Abroad

In addition to state and regional tourism offices, visitors from outside the US may obtain information from the nearest US embassy or consulate in their country of residence (*see partial list below*). For a complete list of American consulates and embassies abroad, see the US State Department Bureau of Consular Affairs listing on the Internet at travel.state.gov.

◆ **Australia**
Moonah Place
Yarralumla, ACT 2600.
02 6214 5600.
canberra.usembassy.gov.

◆ **Canada**
490 Sussex Drive
Ottawa, Ontario K1N 1G8
613-688-5335
canada.usembassy.gov.

◆ **China**
Xiu Shui Bei Jie 3, 100600
86-10 6532-3831
china.usembassy.gov.

◆ **France**
2, avenue Gabriel
75382 Paris Cedex 08
33 1 43 12 22 22
france.usembassy.gov.

◆ **Germany**
Neustädtische Kirchstr
4-5, 10117 Berlin
Federal Republic of Germany
030 2385 174
germany.usembassy.gov.

◆ **Japan**
1-10-5 Akasaka

Minato-ku, Tokyo
107-8420 Japan
03 3224-5000
tokyo.usembassy.gov.

◆ **Mexico**
Paseo de la Reforma
305 Col. Cuauhtemoc
06500 Mexico, D.F.
01-55 5080-2000
mexico.usembassy.gov.

◆ **United Kingdom**
24 Grosvenor Square
London, W1A 1AE
United Kingdom
[44] (0)20 7499-9000
london.usembassy.gov.

Some countries have consular offices in Anchorage. Visitor information centers are indicated on maps in this guide by the 🛈 symbol.

Entry Requirements

All foreign visitors to the US (including Canadian residents and citizens) must present a valid machine-readable passport for entry into the country. Citizens of countries participating in the Visa Waiver Pilot Program (VWPP) are not required to obtain a visa to enter the US for visits of fewer than 90 days. They will, however, be required to furnish a current passport, round-trip ticket and the customs form distributed in the airplane. Travelers from visa-waiver countries who are arriving by air or sea must register at least 10 days prior to travel with the Electronic System for Travel Authorization (ESTA) by supplying personal identification information at the US Department of Homeland Security's website, esta.cbp.dhs.gov/esta. Citizens of countries not participating in the

VWPP must have a visitor's visa. For visa inquiries and applications, contact the nearest US embassy or consulate, or visit the US State Department Visa Services Internet site: travel.state.gov/visa.

Custom Regulations

All articles brought into the US must be declared at time of entry. The following items are exempt from customs regulations: personal effects; one liter of alcoholic beverages (providing visitor is at least 21 years old); either 200 cigarettes, 50 cigars (additional 100 possible under gift exemption) or 2 kilograms of smoking tobacco; and gifts (to persons in the US) not exceeding $100 in value. However, it is best if possible not to bring gifts into either the US or Canada, as customs protocols often require search and inspection of gifts. Prohibited items include firearms and ammunition (if not intended for legitimate sporting purposes); plant materials, meat or poultry products and many other foods. For other prohibited items, exemptions and information, contact any of the following before departure: a US embassy or consulate, Customs Headquarters (*US Customs Service, 1300 Pennsylvania Ave. NW, Washington DC 20229; 202-927-1000*) or the **US Customs Traveler Information** page on the Internet (*www.customs.gov/travel*) Note that most major cities have a local customs port; contact information is available from Customs Headquarters or from the Internet site. In Alaska, customs ports are found in Anchorage, Fairbanks, border entry cities such as Skagway, and ports such as Juneau and Sitka.

Travalers **crossing into Canada** from the US must likewise declare all items being brought into the country. Note that Canada has stringent gun control laws that strictly regulate the import, for whatever purpose (including hunting or personal protection) of all firearms. Do not attempt to bring guns into Canada. In addition, anyone who has ever been arrested may be denied entry, even if no conviction resulted.

Health

The US does not have a national health program; doctors' visits and hospitalization costs may seem high to most visitors. Check with your insurance company to determine if your **medical insurance** covers doctors' visits, medication and hospitalization in the US. If not, it is strongly recommended that you purchase a travel-insurance plan before departing. Many clinics, hospitals, dentists and physicians will not treat walk-in patients—except in emergencies—without cash payment beforehand. Prescription drugs should be properly identified and accompanied by a copy of the prescription.

Safety in the Wild

In most natural areas, tampering with plants or wildlife is dangerous and is prohibited by law. Avoid direct contact with wildlife; any animal that does not shy from humans may be sick. Some wild animals, particularly bears, may approach cars or campsites out of curiosity or if they smell food. *Never offer food to wild animals – not only is this an extremely dangerous action, it is illegal.*

PRACTICAL INFORMATION

If a bear approaches, try to dissuade it by talking calmly and backing away slowly. Never approach a mother with cubs, as she may attack to protect her young. Visitors are required to stay 30 yards from a moose and 300 yards from any bear. Moose actually attack more people in Alaska and can be highly dangerous animals; bear attack fatalities are very rare.

GETTING THERE
By Air

Major US airlines serve most of the West's metropolitan areas. Airports with regular nonstop service to and from European cities include Denver, Dallas-Fort Worth, Houston, Las Vegas, Los Angeles, Phoenix, Portland, San Francisco, and Seattle. For flight information, contact the airline directly.

Virtually all major air service in and to Alaska is provided by **Alaska Airlines** (*www.alaskaair.com*). Most of the time, US airlines attempt to match the fares on the search engine sites such as www. orbitz.com; www.travelocity.com; www.expedia.com. Fare-tracking sites include www.kayak.com.

Major Alaska Airports
Anchorage AK
- **Ted Stevens Anchorage International Airport (ANC)** 907-266-2526 www.dot.alaska.gov/anc.

Fairbanks
- **Fairbanks International Airport (FAI)** 907-474-2500 www.dot.alaska.gov/faiiap.

Juneau
- **Juneau Airport (JNU).** 907-789-7821 www.juneau.org/airport.

Sitka
- **Sitka Rocky Gutierrez Airport (SIT).**

Ketchikan
- **Ketchikan Airport (KTN)** 907-225-6800 www.borough.ketchikan.ak.us.

By Bus

Greyhound, the largest bus company in the US, offers access to most cities and communities, but does not serve Alaska. Travelers to Alaska may want to use Greyhound services to Washington state or to Canada and take other transportation into Alaska. Greyhound offers various passes ranging from 7 days at $285 to 60 days at $650; discounted go-anywhere fares (advance purchase) and other specials and promotions; visit Greyhound's website (*www. greyhound.com*). Schedules, prices and route information: 800-231-2222 (US only) or Greyhound Lines, Inc., P.O. Box 660362, Dallas, TX 75266-0362.

Travel by floatplane
© Travel Juneau

There is a bus service between Anchorage, Fairbanks, and Whitehorse in Canada's Yukon Territory, via **Alaska Direct Bus Line** (*907-277-6652 or 800-770-6652; www.alaskadirectbusline.com*).

By Car

Land entry to Alaska is possible only from Canada, such as the Alaska Highway (*Route 1 in Yukon Territory and Route 97 in British Columbia*) and Route 2 from Whitehorse into Skagway. Alaska's **road system**, though limited, is good—and, much to the surprise of outsiders, is kept open throughout the state all winter—even the Alaska highway through its many wilderness sections, as considerable truck traffic travels the highway year-round. Visitors should note that snow is possible (though rare in summer months) on some portions of roadway throughout the year, such as near the entrance to Denali National Park south of Fairbanks.

By Ship

Ferries – Scheduled ferry service from Bellingham, WA to maritime ports in Alaska, including Juneau, Kodiak, Valdez, Homer and the Aleutians, is provided by the **Alaska Marine Highway System** (*907-465-3941 or 800-642-0066; www.dot.state.ak.us/amhs*), whose nearest ports of call to Anchorage are Seward and Whittier. Alaska state ferries offer comfortable staterooms to passengers, with or without cars, at an added charge, though the budget travelers' tradition of sleeping on the deck continues.

Cruise Ships – *See Cruising Alaska*.

GETTING AROUND
By Train

Alaska Railroad provides one of North America's greatest rail journeys on its route that links Seward, Anchorage, Talkeetna, Denali National Park and Fairbanks (*Jan–Apr weekly; mid-May–mid-Sept daily; winter weekends only*); for schedule and reservations: Alaska Railroad Corp., 907-265-2494 or 800-544-0552; www. alaskarailroad.com. All passenger trains have domed observation viewing cars and dining facilities; conductors offer interpretive narration. Packages and journeys onboard the Alaska Railroad include numerous iterations of stops in Seward, Anchorage, Girdwood (Alyeska Resort) Denali National Park and Fairbanks; trips may be included as part of cruise packages. The railroad is adding whistle stops at several remote locales north and south of Anchorage at which hikers may disembark, spend a day exploring, and reboard a train that evening (*summer only*).

By Ferry

Scheduled ferry service in Alaska is provided by the **Alaska Marine Highway System** (*907-465-3941 or 800-642-0066; www.dot.state. ak.us/amhs*) for Anchorage, Seward, Whittier, Valdez and other communities. Several Alaska Marine Highway routes pass through Prince William Sound on their way to Cordova, Valdez and Whittier. Kodiak Island is also served by Alaska Marine ferries.

By Bus

There is a bus service between Anchorage, Fairbanks and Whitehorse, in Canada's Yukon

Territory, via **Interior Alaska Bus Line** *(907-277-6652 or 800-770-6652; interioralaskabusline.com)*.

Bus service within Anchorage is modest, with the city's **People Mover** designed more for commuters than visitors; www.muni.org/departments/transit.

By Car

All **major highways** in Alaska have both number designations and names. The road between Anchorage and Fairbanks, for instance, is Route 3, the George Parks Highway. The road south from Anchorage to the Kenai Peninsula is the Seward Highway, Routes 1 and 9. There are no interstate highways in Alaska, and most four-lane expressway stretches are found only between Anchorage and Palmer, and around Fairbanks.

Some more remote roads, such as the Dalton Highway from Fairbanks to Deadhorse (Prudhoe Bay) have substantial unpaved stretches, and very few facilities such as gas stations. Consult *The Milepost* Alaska Highway driving guide (which covers most of Alaska; milepost.com) for comprehensive information about highway services along the state's roads.

Rental Cars

National rental companies have offices at major airports and downtown locations. Renters must possess a major credit card and a valid driver's license (international license not required). Minimum age for rental is 25 at most major companies, though younger drivers can often rent by paying a surcharge. All rentals are subject to local taxes and fees which should be included in quoted prices. Liability insurance is not automatically included in the terms of the lease. Be sure to check for proper insurance coverage, offered at an extra charge. Cars may be rented per day, week or month, and mileage is usually unlimited.

Only the person who signed the contract is authorized to drive the rental car, but for an additional fee, and upon presentation of the required papers, additional drivers may be approved. If a vehicle is returned at a different location from where it was rented, drop-off charges may be incurred.

The gasoline tank of the car should be filled before it is returned; rental companies charge a much higher price per gallon than roadside gas stations. Some companies offer a fuel-fill option in which you can "buy" a tank of gas at rental, often at advantageous prices, and return the car with any level of gas in the tank.

Rental car **information and reservations** across the US may be accessed on the Internet (www.bnm.com), or by calling one of the companies listed below.

- **Alamo** – 800-462-5266 www.alamo.com.
- **Avis** – 800-331-1212 www.avis.com.
- **Budget** – 800-527-0700 www.budget.com.
- **Dollar** – 800-800-3665 www.dollar.com.
- **Hertz** – 800-654-3131 www.hertz.com.
- **National** – 800-227-7368 www.nationalcar.com.
- **Thrifty** – 800-331-4200 www.thrifty.com.
- **Enterprise** – 800-261-7331 www.enterprise.com.

Recreational Vehicle (RV) Rentals

One-way rentals range from a basic camper to full-size motorhomes that can accommodate up to seven people and offer a bathroom, shower and kitchen with microwave oven.

Reservations should be made several months in advance. A minimum number of rental days required. A drop fee is charged for one-way rentals.

Cruise America RV (*800-671-8042, www.cruiseamerica.com*) offers rentals with 24hr customer assistance.

The **Recreational Vehicle Rental Association** (RVRA) lists a directory of RV rental locations in the US on their Website (*703-591-7130; www.rvra.org*).

RV America (*www.rvamerica.com*) offers an on-line database of RV rental companies as well as information on campgrounds and RV associations.

Road Regulations

The speed limit on most major highways in Alaska ranges from 50mph (88km/h) to 65mph (105km/h), depending on the location and quality of the road. (Limits drop within urban areas.) Within cities, speed limits are generally 35mph (56km/h), and average 25-30mph (40-48km/h) in residential areas. Headlights must be turned on when driving in fog and rain. Unless traveling on a divided road, the law requires that motorists in both directions bring their vehicle to a full stop when the warning signals on a school bus are activated. Parking spaces identified with ♿ are reserved for persons with disabilities only. Anyone parking in these spaces without proper identification will be ticketed and/or their vehicle will be towed.

The use of **seat belts** is mandatory for all persons in the car. Child safety seats are required in Alaska and are available at most rental-car agencies; indicate need when making reservations. Auto liability insurance is mandatory; if your personal insurance does not cover rental cars, you must purchase coverage from the rental agency.

It is illegal to drink and drive and penalties are severe and may include immediate incarceration and surrender of car and driving license. The maximum blood alcohol content is .08 percent.

In Case of Accident

If you are involved in an auto accident resulting in personal or property damage, you must notify the local police and remain at the scene until dismissed. If blocking traffic, vehicles should be moved to the side of the road as soon as possible, unless serious injury has occurred.

Automobile associations such as the **American Automobile Association (AAA)** provide their members with emergency road service. Members of AAA-affiliated automobile clubs outside the US benefit from reciprocal services. Here's a partial list:

Canada
* **Canadian Automobile Association (CAA)** 613 247 0117

Moose in town

© Roy Neese/Visit Anchorage

United Kingdom

- **The Automobile Association (AA)**
  800 444 999
- **The Royal Scottish Automobile Club (RSAC)**
  141 946 5045

ACCESSIBILITY

Federal law requires that existing businesses (including hotels and restaurants) increase accessibility and provide specially designed accommodations for the disabled. It also requires that wheelchair access, devices for the hearing impaired, and designated parking spaces be available at newly constructed hotels and restaurants. Many public buses are equipped with wheelchair lifts; many hotels have rooms designed for visitors with special needs. Reservations for hand-controlled rental cars should be made well in advance.
All national and most state **parks** have restrooms and other facilities for the disabled (such as wheelchair-accessible nature trails). Permanently disabled US citizens are eligible for a free **US national**

recreational lands pass (*see page 37*) which entitles the carrier to free admission to all national parks and a 50 percent discount on user fees (campsites, boat launches). The pass is available at any national-park entrance fee area with proper proof of disability. For details, contact the National Park Service, Office of Public Inquiries (*1849 C St. NW, Washington DC 20240; 202-208-4747, www.nps.gov*). Many attractions can also make special arrangements for disabled visitors. For information about travel for individuals or groups, contact the **Society for the Advancement of Travel for the Handicapped** (*347 5th Ave., Suite 610, New York, NY 10016; 212-447-7284; www.sath.org*).

BASIC INFORMATION
Accommodations

For a selection of lodgings for cities and regions described in this guide, see **Hotels** at the back of this guide.
Luxury **hotels** are found in Alaska only in Anchorage; **motels** are in clusters on the edges of towns and along major highways. **Bed-**

and-breakfast inns usually are found in residential areas of cities and towns, and in more secluded natural areas. Many properties offer special packages and weekend rates that may not be extended during peak summer months (late May–late Aug) and holiday seasons, especially near major destinations such as Denali National Park. Advance reservations are recommended at all times. Rates are always higher from May 15 to September 15; and, in Anchorage in early March around Iditarod time. Most major hotels include facilities such as business centers, fitness centers, all-day restaurants and, in Anchorage, Juneau, Fairbanks and Sitka, airport shuttles. Activities such as hiking, fishing, mountain biking and wildlife watching may be arranged by contacting hotel staff.

Some cities and communities levy a hotel occupancy tax that is added to hotel rates. Contact local tourist offices to request free information about area accommodations.

Hotels and Motels

Rates for hotels and motels vary greatly according to season and location, and are much higher during holiday and peak seasons (in Alaska, generally summer, except for Northern Lights viewing lodges in the Interior). For deluxe hotels, plan to pay at least $250 and up/night per room, double occupancy. Moderate hotels will charge $100–$250/night and budget motels range from $30–$100/night. In most hotels, children under 18 stay free when sharing a room with their parents. In-room efficiency kitchens are available at some hotels and motels. When reserving, ask about packages including meals, passes to local attractions and weekend specials. Typical amenities at hotels and motels include television, alarm clock, Internet access, smoking/non-smoking rooms, restaurants and airport shuttles. Always advise the reservations clerk of late arrival; unless confirmed with a credit card, rooms may not be held after 6pm.

Reservation Services

Hotel reservation services are abundant, especially on the Internet. Following is a brief selection.

- **Central Reservation Service**
  800-555-7555
  www.reservation-services.com
- **Hotels.com**
  www.hotels.com
- **Quikbook**
  800-789-9887.
  www.quikbook.com

Camping and RV Parks

Alaska campsites are located in national parks, state parks, national forests, along beaches and in private campgrounds. The season for camping usually runs from Memorial Day to Labor Day; in lower elevations, a few campgrounds are open year-round. Some offer full utility hookups, lodges or cabins, backcountry sites and recreational facilities. Advance reservations are recommended, especially during summer and holidays and at popular locales such as Denali National Park. **National park and state park campgrounds** are relatively inexpensive, but fill quickly, especially during school holidays. Facilities range from simple tent sites to RV spaces (*reserve 60 days in* *advance*) or rustic cabins (*reserve one year in advance*). Fees vary according to season and available facilities (picnic tables, water/electric hookups, used-water disposal, recreational equipment, showers, restrooms): camping & RV sites $6–$21/day; cabins $20–$110/day. For all US national parks, national forests, BLM campgrounds and so on, contact the park you are visiting at the federal reservation site, recreation.gov (*518-885-3639 or 877-444-6777; recreation.gov*). For state parks, contact Alaska State Parks (www.alaskastateparks.org) or information.

Private campgrounds offering facilities from simple tent sites to full RV-hookups are plentiful. They are slightly more expensive (*$10–$16/day for tent sites, $20–$45/day for RVs*) but may offer more sophisticated amenities: hot showers, laundry facilities, convenience stores, children's playgrounds, pools, air-conditioned cabins and outdoor recreational facilities. Most accept daily, weekly or monthly occupancy. In winter (*Nov–Apr*), most campgrounds may be closed. Reservations are recommended, especially for longer stays and in popular resort areas. **Kampgrounds of America (KOA)** operates campsites for tents, cabins/cottages and RV-hookups throughout the US. For a directory (*$10 by mail or view online free at www.koakampgrounds.com*), contact KOA Kampgrounds, P.O. Box 30558, Billings MT 59114 (*406-248-7444*). Directories of campgrounds throughout the US are easily found on the Internet and in the Alaska Highway guide *The Milepost*. Here are some Internet **campground directories** covering the US:

- **Camping USA** – www.camping-usa.com
- **CIS' RV-America Travel & Service Center** – www.rv-america.com
- **Go Camping America Directory** – www.gocampingamerica.com
- **RVing Campground Directory** – www.rving.com
- **USA Campgrounds & RV Parks** – usacampgrounds.net

Business Hours

Most businesses operate Mon–Fri 9am–5pm. Banks are normally open Mon–Fri 9am–5:30pm, Sat 10am-1pm. Virtually all bank branches big and small, in cities and towns big and small, now have ATMs operating 24 hours. Most retail stores and specialty shops are open daily 10am–6pm. Malls and shopping centers are usually open Mon–Sat 10am–9pm, Sun 10am–6pm.

Discounts

Many hotels, attractions and restaurants offer discounts to **senior citizens**, with qualifying ages ranging from 55 to 62 (proof of age may be required). Discounts and additional information are available to members of AARP, (*601 E St. N.W. Washington, DC 20094; 202-434-2277, www.aarp.org*), which is open to people over 50.

Electricity

Voltage in the US is 120 volts AC, 60 Hz. Foreign-made appliances may need AC adapters (available at specialty travel and electronics stores) and North American flat-blade plugs.

Emergencies

Except in remote areas where there is little or no telephone service, the emergency phone number throughout Alaska is 911, which can be dialed from any operating phone. Visitors in need of urgent non-emergency medical care can visit the emergency room at the closest hospital or one of many urgent care clinics found in most cities. Patients will likely be required to demonstrate financial ability to pay. Anchorage, Fairbanks and Juneau have local clinics that provide urgent dental care and 24 hour pharmacies.

Internet

High-speed Internet service (Wi-Fi) is available in virtually all hotels and lodges in Alaska, as well as in many restaurants and coffee shops, libraries and visitor centers.

Liquor Laws

The minimum age for purchase and consumption of alcoholic beverages is 21; proof of age may be required. Local municipalities may limit and restrict sales, and laws differ among states. In many states, liquor stores sell beer, wine and liquor. Beer and wine may also be purchased in package-goods stores and grocery stores. It is a serious offense for those over 21 to procure alcohol for minors.

Major Holidays

Banks and government offices are closed on the following legal holidays:
New Year's Day: *January 1*
Martin Luther King Jr.'s Birthday*: *3rd Monday in January*
President's Day*: *3rd Monday in February*
Memorial Day*: *last Monday in May*
Independence Day: *July 4*
Labor Day*: *1st Monday in September*
Columbus Day*: *2nd Monday in October*
Veterans Day*: *November 11*
Thanksgiving Day: *4th Thursday in November*
Christmas Day: *December 25*
*Many retail stores and restaurants stay open on these days.

Mail

First-class postage rates within the US are: 47¢/letter (*up to 1oz*) and 34¢/postcard. Overseas rates are based on recipient country. Most post offices are open Mon–Fri 9am–5pm; some may open Sat 9am–noon. Companies such as UPS-Mail Boxes Etc. and FedexKinko's also provide mail service for everything from postcards to large packages. These companies also sell boxes and other packaging material. For photocopying, fax service and computer access, FedexKinko's has locations throughout the US (*800-254-6567, www.kinkos.com*) or consult the yellow pages in a local phone book under Copying Service for a listing of local companies.

Money

The American **dollar** ($1) is divided into 100 **cents**. A **penny** = 1 cent (1¢); a **nickel** = 5¢; a **dime** = 10¢; a **quarter** = 25¢.
Most national banks and Thomas Cook (*locations throughout the US, 800-287-7362; www.thomascook.com*) **exchange foreign currency** at local offices and charge a fee for the service. Currency exchange is also available in most major airports, including Anchorage; and at some major banks in large cities.

Other methods to obtain dollars are to use traveler's checks (*usually accepted only in banks and hotels, with presentation of a photo ID*) or to withdraw cash from **ATMs** (Automated Teller Machines) with a debit or credit card. Banks charge a fee (*$1–$3*) for non-members who use their ATMs. For more information on the ATM network, call MasterCard/Cirrus (*800-424-7787*) or Visa/Plus System (*800-843-7587*). In the event you lose your credit card, immediately call your care provider: American Express, 800-528-4800; Diner's Club, 800-234-6377; MasterCard/ Eurocard, 800-307-7309; Visa/Carte Bleue, 800-336-8472.

It is also possible to send and receive cash via **Western Union** (*locations in more than 100 countries, 800-325-6000, www.westernunion.com*).

Smoking

Like the rest of the US West, Alaska and its cities have imposed substantial restrictions on public smoking, inaugurating protections for nonsmokers so extensive that one sees smokers huddled outside in temperatures far below zero in winter. Laws vary, but it is illegal to smoke in public areas in most places such as restaurants, airports, buses, and offices open to the public such as banks and retail stores. All US airlines are completely nonsmoking, as are ferries and railroads. A few Alaska hotels still offer a smattering of smoking rooms, but this is rare and declining.

For a complete state-by-state list of restrictions, consult Action on Smoking and Health, www.ash.org. Aside from legal restrictions, it is socially unacceptable to expose other individuals to tobacco smoke. Virtually all smokers voluntarily retire to locations where their habit will not affect others. If you are bothered by someone's smoke, it is quite all right to ask them to move, unless you are in a private residence or designated smoking area.

Taxes and Tipping

Although Alaska has no **sales tax**, some cities charge one. There are also tourism taxes such as a bed tax, a small surcharge on cruise passengers, airport fees and surcharges on travel to Alaska. In restaurants, it is customary to leave the server a **gratuity, or tip**, of 10–20 percent of the total bill (since it almost never is included otherwise). Taxi drivers are generally tipped 15 percent of the fare. Hotel bellhops and courtesy bus drivers are tipped $1-$2 and housekeeping $1-$2 per night. On cruises, it is customary to leave cabin stewards a tip of $5-$10 a night before disembarking the ship. Many visitors feel it's appropriate to tip tour guides.

Telephones

For **long-distance** calls in the US and Canada, dial 1 + area code

Important Phone Numbers	
Emergency (police, fire department)	☏911
Directory Assistance	☏411

(3 digits) + number (7 digits). Note: Many cellular phones, depending on the service provider, do not require the initial 1; just dial the 10-digit number you wish to call. To place **local calls**, dial the seven-digit number without 1 or the area code, unless the local calling area includes several area codes. To place an **international call**, dial 011 + country code + area code + number. To obtain help from an **operator**, dial 0 for local and 00 for long distance. For **information** on a number within your area code, dial 411. For long-distance information, dial 1 + area code + 555-1212. To place **collect calls**, dial 0 + area or country code + number. At the operator's prompt, give your name. For all **emergencies**, dial **911**.

Since most **hotels** add a surcharge for local and long-distance calls, it is preferable to use your calling card or cell phone. Local calls from public telephones cost 50¢ unless otherwise posted.

Public telephones accept quarters, dimes and nickels and credit cards. You may also use your calling card or credit card (recommended for long-distance calls to avoid the inconvenience of depositing large amounts of change). Instructions for using public telephones are listed on or near the phone.

Cell phone coverage is widespread in and around cities, towns and popular tourist attractions in Alaska (such as the Denali National Park entrance), but it remains sketchy or even nonexistent in remote areas. Coverage varies with different carriers, but most phones have full service in cities and towns.

Toll-free – The telephone area code throughout Alaska is 907. Unless otherwise indicated, telephone numbers that start with **800, 888, 877** and **866** are toll-free within the US, and often Canada. European travelers may find that their phone service provider does not offer connection to US toll-free numbers; if so, call the direct number (in Alaska all such numbers begin with area code 907) instead. Numbers that begin with 900 charge extra fees, sometimes exorbitant; do not use these.

Time Zones

The Alaska time zone is four hours later than New York, and covers the entire state except for the far western Aleutian Islands. Daylight Saving Time is observed from mid-March to mid-November: time is moved forward one hour, bringing a later dawn but also a later dusk. Alaska Standard Time (PST) is 9hrs behind Greenwich Mean Time (GMT), or Universal Time (UT).

ADVENTURE TRAVEL

Alaska's largely undeveloped and implacably wild landscape provides unlimited opportunities for outdoor adventure—from fishing in the Kenai and kayaking in Prince William Sound to cross-country skiing near Talkeetna with the shimmering pinnacle of Denali in the background.

Organized Tours

Contact local tourism offices (*p 23*) for information about activities in specific geographic areas, or consider an organized tour. **REI** a Seattle-born co-op, offers an extensive catalog of tours and

Kayaking in Alaska's open waters

© Travel Juneau

operates a store in Anchorage. **REI** also offers an extensive catalog of trips and adventures: www.rei.com.

Guides and Outfitters

Outdoor adventure in Alaska is best pursued by visitors with the help of experienced guides and outfitters. The state's climate, ample wildlife, vast wilderness and sparse development mean expertise is essential.

All but the most experienced **white-water rafters and kayakers** book expert guides to lead them through rivers' perils. The most popular rafting trips in Alaska are just outside Denali National Park along the **Nenana River**; outfitters include Denali Raft Adventures (*www.denaliraft.com*) and Denali Outdoor Center (*www. denalioutdoorcenter.com*).

For a list of outfitters and guides, the state travel agency maintains a list of adventure providers at www.travelalaska.com. A list of accredited **mountaineering organizations** can be obtained from the nonprofit **American Mountain Guides Association** (*710 Tenth St., Suite 101, Golden CO 80401; 303-271-0984, www.amga.com*).

America Outdoors (*P.O. Box 10847, Knoxville TN 37939; 865-558-3595, www.americaoutdoors.org*) offers an outfitter database on its website and a free publication available by mail that lists US outfitters.

Tour Providers

Following is a sampling of tour providers and programs:

For exciting **all–inclusive vacations** involving activities such as bicycling, hiking and kayaking, contact **Backroads** (*801 Cedar St., Berkeley CA 94710-1800; 510-527-1555 or 800-462-2848, www.backroads.com*).

Programs include destinations in Alaska, Arizona, California, Colorado, Hawaii, Idaho, Montana, New Mexico, Utah, Washington and Wyoming.

Multi-sport vacations are available from **The World Outdoors** (*2840 Wilderness Place, Suite F, Boulder CO 80301; 303-413-0938 or 800-488-8483, www.theworld*

MUST KNOW

outdoors.com). Destinations include Alaska, Arizona, California, Colorado, Hawaii, Montana, New Mexico, Utah and Wyoming.

Covering the western US from Alaska to Arizona, **Austin-Lehman Adventures** (*P.O. Box 81025, Billings MT 59108-1025; 406-586-3556 or 800-575-1540, www.austinlehman.com*) provides multi-sport vacations. **John Hall's Alaska Cruises and Tours** (*1127 North Lakeshore Dr., Lake City, MN 55041; 800–325–2270; kissalaska.com*) is a boutique tour company that specializes in expert, curated small-group journeys throughout Alaska; they encompass both the state's natural wonders and parks, and its thriving Native cultures. Tours range from Barrow to Ketchikan, and utilize coaches and small cruise ships.

Historic Trails

The National Park Service, US Forest Service and Bureau of Land Management administer national scenic and national historic trails in the US. Some are designated for hikers, others (historic) for car travelers.

For information, obtain the National Trails System Map and Guide (*$1.25*) from the Consumer Information Center, US General Services Administration (*Pueblo CO 81009; 800-333-4636, www.pueblo.gsa.gov*) or contact the agencies listed below.

National Trails System Branch of the National Park Service 1849 C St. NW, Washington DC 20240, 202-565-1177, www.nps.gov/nts.

Iditarod National Historic Trail Iditarod Trail Committee, 907-376-5155. www.iditarod.com.

National & State Lands

The vast majority of Alaska is public property—more than two-thirds of the state's land is still owned by the US government, including national parks, and wildlife refuges, all of which offer year-round recreational opportunities. US federal land-management agencies support a comprehensive online database (*www.recreation.gov*) that supplies information on all recreation areas through search options and Internet links. The **National Park Service** lists all lands under its jurisdiction on its website (*www.nps.gov*). Unique to Alaska are four cooperative information centers that guide visitors to the state's federal and state public lands. Public Lands Information Centers in Anchorage, Fairbanks, Ketchikan and Tok are open weekdays and include interpretive displays as well as adventure information (*alaskacenters.gov*). Both national and state parks offer **season passes**. The US national recreational lands pass (*$80*) is valid for one year and includes admission to all national parks and other federal lands that charge admission, parking fees and so on. The pass may be purchased at any park entrance or online at www.nps.gov. Most parks have information centers equipped with trail maps and informative literature on park facilities and activities.

Alaska Regional Office, National Park Service. www.nps.gov/akso. **Alaska Division of Parks & Outdoor Recreation**. www.dnr.state.ak.us/parks.

THE LAST FRONTIER

Spanning 2,350mi from the Canadian border to the Aleutian Islands, the 49th state juts out into the Pacific Ocean at the northwestern corner of North America. Separated from Siberia by less than 60mi of water, this Land of the Midnight Sun neighbors Canada's Yukon Territory and sits 500mi northwest of the nearest US mainland state of Washington. More than twice the size of Texas, Alaska boasts the 16 highest peaks in the US, an estimated 10,000 glaciers, and 3.3 million acres of state parks. Only 736,000 people reside in this huge state of 570,640sq mi, ranking it the last in terms of population density. Bears and whales, eagles and seals, moose and caribou roam the land, air and water. Ancient forests, vast tundras and snowy peaks vie for attention. Hardy adventurers carve wilderness toeholds and sift gold from remote streams, and equally hardy fishermen brave powerful seas for crab, salmon, halibut and more.

Even today independent **gold miners** run small operations in the Alaska bush—but the state holds more intriguing facets that expand its appeal beyond untrammeled nature and unfettered people. Here three superb **museums** boast world-class collections of aboriginal art. The largest city, **Anchorage**, is a cosmopolitan urban area with excellent restaurants, nightclubs, theaters and what may be the best recreational **trail network** in the US. Travelers seeking deeper understanding of our changing world can visit **glaciers** whose rapid shrinkage bears unmistakable evidence of climate change. Fans of **indigenous cultures** can enjoy a resurgence of Native song, dance, chant, art and culture.

The age-old urge to see and settle new lands first brought humans to what is essentially a subcontinent more than 10,000 years ago. A global ice age lowered ocean levels, and opened a land bridge across the **Bering Strait** between Siberia and Alaska. Migrants streamed across it—in several waves that may date back more than 20,000 years, some

Fast Facts

Land area: 570,640sq mi (1.52 million sq km), bigger than all European countries except Russia

Population: 736,000 people (48 percent female), 900,000 caribou, 135,000 bears and 200,000 moose

Permanent fund dividend paid each resident: $2, 072 (2015)

Largest city: Anchorage, with a population of 295,570

Capital: Juneau

Alaskans with pilot's license: 8,165—more than Massachusetts, which has nine times as many residents

Annual visitors: 2 million

anthropologists now believe; and may have also included boat-borne migrations when the land bridge was beneath the sea.

Here these early settlers found rich seafood resources, ample wild game and limitless land. Over the millennia these migrants spread south across North America; those who stayed in Alaska differentiated into at least two dozen distinct peoples in four broad groups: the interior **Athabaskans**; the coastal peoples of Southeast Alaska; the **Aleuts**; and the subarctic and Arctic coastal **Inupiaq** and **Yup'ik**. Adapting to the harsh conditions, these peoples relied on foods from land and sea ranging from whales to tiny eulachons (anchovies); constructed houses ranging from huge cedar plank longhouses in Southeast Alaska to the famous ice-block igloos of the Arctic; and whiled away the long winter nights developing rich traditions of song, chant, dance and storytelling.

In 1741 Danish navigator **Vitus Bering**, commissioned by the czar of Russia, set sail for southern Alaska. On the return voyage, his ship ran aground off the Siberian coast. Encouraged by the sea otter

Naming Rights

The name "Alaska" is derived from "Alyeska," an archaic transcription of an Aleut word that means "great land of white to the east." Thus the state's informal nickname is the "Great Land." Officially, its nickname is "Last Frontier."

pelts surviving crew members brought back, Russian fur traders began plying Alaskan waters, largely around the Aleutian Islands. Spanish explorers appeared later in the same century, one of whom sailed into Sitka Sound and claimed the region for Spain. But the latter did little to solidify its claim, and the first **Russian settlement** was established on Kodiak Island in 1784. With the creation of the Russian-American Company in 1799, and the boom in demand for sea otter pelts, Alaska became a full-fledged Russian colony. Sitka became the capital, after Russian forces under Alexander Baranov defeated the Tlingits at the Battle of Sitka in 1804. Voracious trapping drove sea otters to near extinction, and

Kodiak Village, Harriman Expedition, 1899

©U.S. Geological Survey

THE LAST FRONTIER

The decline of the fur trade coupled with a crippling loss in the Crimean War (1853-56) spelled the end of Russia's tenure on Alaska soil. Russia began meetings with US Secretary of State William Seward in 1866 to discuss selling off Alaska. In October 1867 the Russian flag came down and the *Stars and Stripes* went up. Editorials lambasted the deal, calling the area a worthless piece of real estate and tagging it Seward's Folly and Seward's Icebox. In Alaska, the Tlingits raisied a shame pole for his failure to reciprocate a welcome feast in his honor *(see Saxman Village)*. For the next two decades, Congress ignored its new purchase. Not until 1884 were federal district courts and a school program set up. Private companies had gone ahead and built canneries, initiating a salmon industry that would become the world's largest. Discoveries of gold in 1880 proved that fish were not the only riches in this "worthless piece" of land.

the trade collapsed. Russia sold all of its Alaska possessions to the US in 1867, a $7.2 million purchase long known as **Seward's Folly** *(see sidebar)* until the **discovery of gold** in the late 19C, which fueled a quarter-century boom in Alaska. Though the lower 48 states had considered Alaska a frozen wasteland, the glitter of gold swelled development with rushes in Juneau (1880), Skagway and the Klondike (1897-98), Nome (1899) and Fairbanks (1902). The territory fell into obscurity, though, until World War II made it an American front line in the Pacific Theater. Completed in 1942, the **Alaska Highway** linked Canada and the lower 48 states to Fairbanks through 1,500mi of wilderness. Constructed, incredibly, in only eight months, it was the first land-transport connection between Alaska and the rest of North America.

US statehood in 1959 brought recognition of the state's riches and strategic importance, as well as the need to grapple with a complex web of Native claims, developers' interests

and conservationists' concerns. Development of the North Slope petroleum industry climaxed in 1977 with the completion of the **Trans-Alaska Pipeline**, which brings oil from Prudhoe Bay to Valdez for shipment "outside," as Alaskans call the rest of the world. Despite fierce opposition in the state, the 1980 Alaska National Interest Lands Conservation Act provided federal protection to more than 100 million acres of land, and created or expanded 15 national parks and preserves. Unique in the country, Alaska's federal parks and preserves are open to subsistence hunting. Today, Alaska represents outstanding superlatives in the American pantheon. It's as big as Texas, California and Montana combined (Anchorage alone is almost as big as Delaware). It has 33,904mi of coastline, 3,000 rivers and 3 million lakes. The Great Land contains almost two-thirds—54 million acres— of US national parklands, including the **largest single park**, Wrangell St. Elias, whose 13.2 million acres alone equal almost half the area

© Lark Carlson Brown/Bigstockphoto.com

Anchorage Bay and Chugach Mountains

encompassed by national parks elsewhere in the country. Alaska's state parks total some 3.3 million acres, the greatest in the US. The state holds the largest national forest, the Tongass.

In terms of **the economy**, the state is America's second-largest gold producer, second-greatest producer of crude oil, and producer of as much seafood as all other 49 states combined. The state's oldest craft brewing company and gourmet coffee roaster, both in Juneau, date back to the 1980s, long before such products were common in the Lower 48.

But quantitative superlatives serve only as the foundation for a fascinating place. The rugged **pioneer ethos** survives in Alaska today as in few other places around the world. Most born-and-bred Alaskans are raised on moose steaks, salmon and caribou sausage, rather than hamburgers, hot dogs and canned tuna. Usually fairly conservative, Alaska—the launchpad for Sarah Palin—is nonetheless one of just four US states to prohibit billboards (it's one of the key reasons the landscape is so scenic). Visitors can experience the wildlife, wild land and hardy people as well as the gourmet food, palpable cultural climate, and sophisticated travel industry. Few places on earth are anything like Alaska: Alaskans would say, no other place on earth. It's easy to agree with them.

"Uncle" Ted Stevens

Appointed to the House of Representatives in 1968, then elected outright in 1970, Theodore Fulton Stevens (1923-2010) became the longest serving Republican senator in US history. During his 40-year Senate career, he left his mark on so much of the state, from his support for the Alaska Native Claims Settlement Act to his opposition to legislation affording federal protection to much of Alaska. Highways, tunnels, military bases, airports, universities and federal buildings—virtually everything in Alaska bears the Stevens touch, thus his nickname "Uncle Ted." In 2000 he was named "Alaskan of the Century" by a statewide committee. In 2008 he was convicted of corruption, and lost his seat in Congress. The conviction was thrown out on appeal a year later, but Stevens died in a plane crash in 2010.

THE LAST FRONTIER

JUNEAU★

Alaska's capital is famous as the country's only state capital not reachable by road from the rest of its state. It's also the only capital whose state residents voted to move it (in 1974)—and then voted to bar funds for the move (1982). Though the subject has come up many times since, Juneau area legislators have always managed to block it— an apt reflection of the fierce loyalty Juneau residents bear for their city and borough.

Founded in 1880 after Joe Juneau and Richard Harris discovered gold in a nearby gulch—following directions from a Tlingit chief—the town became a leading **gold mining** area in North America. Named the territorial capital in 1906, having surpassed the original capital of Sitka, the city grew up along the Gastineau Channel, shouldered by steep mountains on either side. Mining declined by World War II, but remote mines still operate nearby, and proposals recur to reopen more; tourism and government are the main industries. Cruise ships bring close to 1 million visitors each summer to Juneau, a number that makes some of the city's 31,000 residents feel a bit overwhelmed.

The **State Capitol** itself is a nondescript, vaguely Art Deco building downtown. Clay murals in the lobby celebrate the state's fisheries, timber and mineral resources; the rest is given over to offices and legislative chambers. Countless proposals to engineer a road to Juneau from Skagway have neither come to fruition nor disappeared entirely, despite the profound difficulties—the highway would cross almost 90 slide paths, and cost more than $300 million. The idea was revived in 2012—but, like the perennial attempts to move the capital into Alaska's main section, it's still just an idea.

Juneau's South Franklin Street

© Travel Juneau

Practical Information

When to Go

Heavy snow is rare in Juneau. Milder weather often arrives in mid-April, lasting into September. Juneau fans often advise the best time to visit is mid-April to late May. However, as local residents say, an all-around forecast that is good for almost any day of the year is "Partly cloudy, chance of showers." Rain gear is essential.

Getting There

♦ **By Air** – It's 900 air miles northwest of Seattle and 570 air miles southeast of Anchorage to Juneau International Airport (JNU).

Alaska Airlines provides most service from outside Southeast; www.alaskaair.com.

♦ **By Ferry** – Alaska Marine Highway system; www.dot.state.ak.us.

Visitor Information

Visitor centers (open year-round daily per airplane and boat arrivals) are located at Juneau airport and the ferry terminal (13319 Glacier Hwy). Seasonal centers are located downtown (Marine Park, 144 Marine Way, open for ship arrivals) and at the cruise ship terminal (daily 9am–5pm) in summer. 907-586-2201 or 888-581-2201. www.traveljuneau.com.

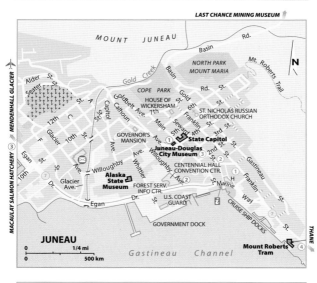

HOTELS		RESTAURANTS	
Alaska's Capital Inn	(1)	Heritage Coffee Co.	(1)
Four Points Sheraton	(2)	Rookery (The)	(2)
Pearson's Pond Luxury Inn	(3)	Salt	(3)
		Twisted Fish Co.	(4)

JUNEAU

MUSEUMS

Alaska State Museum★★★

395 Whittier St. Open May–mid-Sept daily 9am–5pm. Rest of the year Tue–Sat 10am–4pm. $12, winter $5. 907-465-2901. museums.alaska.gov.

This newly expanded (2016) facility is an architectural and cultural gem, more than doubled in size at a cost of $139 million. Collection highlights range from priceless Alaska Native artifacts to the desk on which William Seward supposedly signed the 1867 treaty by which the US bought Alaska from Russia for $7.2 million. Key exhibits include a repatriated **Tlingit frog hat★★**, ownership of which is shared between the state and the Kik.sadi clan; a massive 34ft **umiak★** used for whale and seal hunting; and a complete section of the **Alaska Pipeline** standing erect in the exhibit hall. Other artifacts on display include Athabaskan beadwork, pioneer homestead furnishings, and a full-size example of the famous sailboats from which commercial fishermen once caught Bristol Bay salmon. A large map on the floor of the entrance atrium helps visitors grasp Alaska's immensity. Other exhibits depict Alaska's Gold Rush and World War II history. Upstairs, in the state library, an exquisite 40ft **glass screen★★** by Ketchikan artist Evon Zerbetz depicts the state's human and natural environment in vivid color.

Juneau-Douglas City Museum★

155 S. Seward St. Open May–Sept Mon–Fri 9am-6pm, Sat–Sun 10am–5pm. Rest of the year Tue–Sat 10am–4pm. $6 (free in winter). 907-586-3572. www. juneau.org/parkrec/museum.

Though small, this municipal facility offers intriguing exhibits closely tabbed to life in Southeast Alaska—one devoted to mining technology, for example. The highlight is a historic, woven willow **First Nations fish trap★** preserved in remarkable condition, as it was buried in gravel and mud for centuries. The name reflects the fact that Douglas, a separate

Alaska State Museum's new library, archives and museum building

© Lara Swimmer/Alaska State Museum

Juneau-Douglas City Museum

©Juneau-Douglas City Museum

Last Chance Mining Museum

1001 Basin Rd. $4. Open mid-May–late Sept daily 9:30am–12:30pm and 3:30pm–6:30pm. 907-586-5338. Access to the museum involves a short, but steep hike uphill.

There is no shortage of mining museums in Alaska. What distinguishes the interesting Last Chance Mining Museum is its utterly authentic site—it occupies old mine buildings decommissioned in 1944. From 1912 until it closed, this working mine was the largest hard-rock gold mine on earth.

Most impressive is the stupendous heft of the machinery on hand, including a huge **air compressor**, one of the largest ever built. Hopeful gold-seekers can still pan in the creek below.

town across Gastineau Channel from south Juneau, was a thriving mine center until a catastrophic tunnel inundation in 1917 virtually wiped it out. An interactive display illustrates how the **Treadwell Mine collapse** erased what had been the world's largest gold mine.

FOR FUN

🚡 Mount Roberts Tram★★

490 S. Franklin St. Open May–Sept Mon noon–9pm, Tue–Sun 8am–9pm. $33. 907-463-3412 or 888-820-2628. mountrobertstramway.com.

Owned and operated by Goldbelt, one of Alaska's powerful but low-profile Native corporations, this conveyance offers a dizzying ride that rises from sea level to 1,745ft along a steep slope (68 percent grade) on its namesake mountain. Its base on the waterfront lies conveniently just a short walk from Juneau's cruise ship terminal. The **views★★** provided by the ride are splendid—party because there are no intermediate towers along its

© Travel Juneau

Mount Roberts Tram

path. Except for the ever-thrilling flight into Juneau airport, this vantage point provides the best overlook of Juneau, Gastineau Channel and the area's many towering peaks, all the way north to (on clear days) the forbidding summits of the Wrangell-St. Elias Mountains. Hiking trails on top offer an opportunity to stroll the subalpine woodlands; bears and moose are common sights. The 🐟 **gift shop** is an excellent place to buy authentic Native crafts and art.

Macaulay Salmon Hatchery★

2697 Channel Dr. Open May–Sept Mon–Fri 10am–6pm, Sat–Sun 10am–5pm. $5. 907-463-4810. www.dipac.net.

Fish farming is illegal in Alaska—all fish harvested in the state grow up in open waters in the wild. But hatcheries have been established to boost salmon numbers; this hatchery exemplifies the practice. When it was constructed in 1989, salmon numbers were declining in the region.

Today, more than 114 million salmon—largely chum and coho—are incubated and released to the ocean here every year. A local fishermen's nonprofit corporation operates the hatchery, in which an interpretive center explains the process, as well as the life cycle of North Pacific salmon.

More than a dozen **aquariums★** hold 150 local marine animals; one highlight is a fearsome-looking wolf eel. A touch tank allows visitors to feel sea anemones, seastars and other marine life.

THE GREAT OUTDOORS

Mendenhall Glacier★★★

8510 Mendenhall Loop Rd., 18mi northwest of Juneau via Egan Dr. and Mendenhall Loop Rd. Visitor center open Mon 11:30am–7:30pm, Tue–Sun 8am–7:30pm; rest of the year Thu–Sun 10am–4pm; $3 entry early May–late Sept. 907-789-0097. www.fs.fed.us/r10/tongass/districts.

This famous glacier is the most visited glacier in the US—by 500,000 spectators a year, according to federal managers' estimates. No wonder, given its splendidly scenic framework, its blue-gray-ivory tongue spilling out of a long valley between rock flanks into a sparkling lake. The 12mi river of ice flows down from the 1,500sq-mi Juneau Icefield in the coastal mountains above. Massive waterfalls at the side mark outfall from a neighboring valley. Rare migratory birds, bears and beavers are commonly seen near the glacier. Like virtually all Alaska glaciers, the Mendenhall is in retreat, losing 200-500ft a year, 2.5mi since the mid-1700s. When the visitor center was first built in 1962, it sat very close to the toe of the glacier; now it is quite distant. Despite the Mendenhall's retreat, **glacier treks★★** are a popular outdoor option for Juneau visitors. Experienced guides with **Above & Beyond Alaska** (*7.5hr trips $189;*

Retreating Rivers of Ice

The overall statistics regarding glaciers in Alaska are impressive. The state holds an estimated 10,000 of these rivers of ice, encompassing as much as 29,000sq mi (slightly larger than Austria) with a total volume of 30,000 cubic miles, scientists estimate. Sounds immense, until you consider that Alaska has less than 1 percent of all ice on earth. (The majority is in Antarctica, with about 10 percent in Greenland.)

Alaska's glaciers are almost all found in the steep mountains rimming the Gulf of Alaska. Here, North Pacific storms collide with the mountains and dump immense quantities of snow— hundreds of feet each winter. The key to formation of glacial ice is not sheer cold, but sheer volume of snow, which compacts over time into crystalline ice. (There are few if any glaciers in the polar deserts of Arctic Alaska.) Glaciers flow downhill because of gravity and the pressure of the extreme weight in the icefields where most originate—rather like squeezing toothpaste from a tube. Glaciologists use the term "viscous" to describe this plasticity. Downhill flow ranges from several hundred feet a year to, rarely, hundreds of feet a *day*.

But when the glaciers melt back at a rate faster than they flow down, they "recess"—that is, retreat: the toe of the glacier is backing up despite the continuing flow from above. Virtually all of Alaska's glaciers are recessing, except a few notable examples such as the massive Hubbard Glacier in Yakutat Bay. For a comprehensive academic overview of glacial decline, visit *www.extremeicesurvey.org*.

907-364-2333; *www.beyondak.com*) take hikers around Mendenhall Lake up to the glacier, outfit guests with crampons and ice axes, and lead them onto the ice for an astounding hour-long journey past crevasses, melt-ponds, ice caves and blue ice colored so deeply it is hard to fathom.

© Travel Juneau
Mendenhall Glacier and Nugget Falls

Glacier Bay
National Park ★★

40mi north of Juneau—no direct road access. Direct air service to Gustavus is available from Juneau on Alaska Airlines (summer only), www.alaskaair.com; and on SeaPort Airlines, www.seaport.com. Park visitor center at Bartlett Cove, 1 Park Rd., Gustavus. 907-697-2230. www.nps.gov/glba.
Tours (8hrs) by boat depart each morning from Bartlett Cove. Bring warm clothes, rain gear and binoculars. Lunch is provided.

Famed worldwide as a place where avid glacier-watchers can see rivers of ice calve (shed blocks into the water), this long, mountain-ringed fjord and its tributary valleys offer stunning testament to climate change as well. When explorer George Vancouver sailed by in 1794, there was no bay to be seen at all—ice came all the way to Icy Strait. The ice has been receding ever since, almost 70mi in total. Nowadays a daylong cruise (or passage aboard big cruise ships) is needed to reach the glaciers in Glacier Bay.

While tour operators in Juneau offer day trips to Glacier Bay, the vast majority of non-cruise visitors climb aboard boats operated by park concessionaire Glacier Bay Lodge & Tours, Inc. in Gustavus (*$195; 907-697-4000 or 888-229-8687; www.visitglacierbay.com*). The unforgettable **day-long cruise★★** departs each morning from Bartlett Cove and takes visitors past sea lion haul-outs and mountain goat habitat before reaching the far end of Tarr Inlet near two tidewater glaciers, where everyone waits with bated breath to see if the glacier will calve.

The only accommodation in the park is Bartlett Cove's **Glacier Bay Lodge**, which has functional rooms, a store and marina.

The new (2016) **Huna Tribal House★★★** is an exceptional longhouse at Bartlett Cove that provides a window into Native Tlingit culture. Lodgings and services are available in **Gustavus** (*gustavusak.com*) nearby.

Cruise ship approaching Margerie Glacier, Glacier Bay National Park

© NPS

SOUTHEAST ALASKA★★

By almost every measure, the rugged islands—more than 2,000—and mainland shores of Southeast Alaska are in a different world from the rest of the state. Often called "The Panhandle," Southeast reaches out like an appendage from the body of Alaska toward the lower 48 states, separating Canada from the Gulf of Alaska. Harborside towns, saltwater activities and coniferous rain forest dominate here; the towering peaks of the various coastal ranges top out at Mount St. Elias' 18,000ft and largely block Arctic air from the north. Until recently, several palm trees grew in Sitka. The Tongass National Forest that encompasses much of the region is the nation's largest, an incredible 17 million acres. That's 26,562sq mi, bigger than 10 states in the Lower 48. Sturdy ancient Sitka spruce trees approach millennial age; sea lions, seals, eagles, whales and other maritime creatures dot the air and water; haunting hand-carved totems honor the spirits of the land that First Nations people have cherished for thousands of years.

And what's with the jagged, completely haphazard-looking **boundary** that runs through the mountains between Alaska and Canada? It approximates the line along the mountain summits, or 10 leagues (about 35mi) from the main saltwater shoreline. It represents the boundary the Russians and Britons negotiated in 1825, when European powers thought the only thing of value in the region was sea otter fur. When **gold** was found in the nearby Yukon in 1896, the border gained crucial importance. Boundary disputes continued until the US, inheritor of the Russian claims, and Canada, Britain's successor, settled things through arbitration in 1903. Ironically, then as now the roughly 600mi-long border is virtual wilderness, crossed by just the three roads.

So despite the ready air service into most locales, the ferries and ships that carry thousands up and down the **Inside Passage★★**, the Southeast retains a palpable aura of separation that adds to its already considerable geographic and cultural allure.

Touring Tip

One segment of the tourism market dominates: of the roughly 2 million visitors to Alaska each year, more than half—just past 1 million—are **cruise ship** travelers. The vast majority of those ships sail through Juneau, Ketchikan, Sitka—all have docks for the multi-thousand-passenger liners that mostly depart from Seattle and Vancouver. While the descriptions of cities and attractions herein are meant for travelers of any sort, many of these sights are subject, late May to late September, to mid-morning arrival of hundreds of visitors off-loaded from cruise ships onto tour buses. If you can, it's best to visit sights like Mendenhall Glacier before 10am. The rest of the year, the Southeast is a quiet landscape of raw, rain-dappled beauty.

Practical Information

When to Go

Southeast Alaska has a temperate **maritime climate** year-round. Sitka gets less snowfall than Boston. Late May to late September brings warmer weather, but also hundreds of cruise-ship passengers each day. If you don't like crowds, visit in early May, or even late April, when winter's chill is ebbing. Most attractions are not open every day from October to April, though. Rain occurs throughout the year, so bring rain gear.

Getting There and Around

Save for roads into Skagway and Haines from the Yukon (and a tiny spur into tiny Hyder), the Southeast is reached only by boat or plane.

♦ **By Air** – The main gateway is **Juneau International Airport** (JNU) *(907-789-7821; www.juneau.org/airport)*, which has daily jet service to and from Seattle and Anchorage, and connections to Sitka, Ketchikan, Yakutat and other towns. **Alaska Airlines** *(800-252-7522; www.alaskaair.com)* offers most flights to and from Juneau, with multiple daily flights between the capital and Seattle and Anchorage. Local airlines include **Wings of Alaska** *(907-789-0790 or 800-789-9464; www.wingsofalaska.com)*, which offers service to Gustavus (Glacier Bay), Skagway, Haines, Hoonah and Excursion Inlet; and **Alaska Seaplane Services** *(907-789-3331; www.flyalaskaseaplanes.com)* which operates from the seaplane base next to the main airport and flies to several remote hamlets in the region.

Other major airports with scheduled daily passenger jet service include Sitka (SIT), Ketchikan (KTN) and Yakutat (YAK). Flights to and from these cities often include brief stops at other cities in Southeast; travelers may find themselves on "Combi" Boeing 737s, in which the front third of the plane is devoted to cargo, not just the bottom hold.

♦ **By Ferry** – Scheduled ferry service from Bellingham WA to Juneau and other ports in Southeast Alaska, including Sitka, Ketchikan, Gustavus (Glacier Bay) and Skagway, is provided by the **Alaska Marine Highway System** *(www.dot.state. ak.us)*. Juneau is a very busy cruise ship stop; the vast majority of visitors arrive onboard these behemoths, which tie up at a dock just south of downtown. Similar circumstances pertain in Ketchikan, whose dock is directly downtown on Front Street; and in Sitka, which has a cruise dock north of town about 10min by car, and an anchoring area just below downtown, from which cruise passengers are lightered to shore.

♦ **By Car** – Southeast Alaska can be reached by vehicle on highways from Whitehorse in the Yukon, to Skagway and Haines; both roads intersect with the famous Alaska Highway. The drive from Seattle to either city is more than 1,500mi and requires at least 3 days.

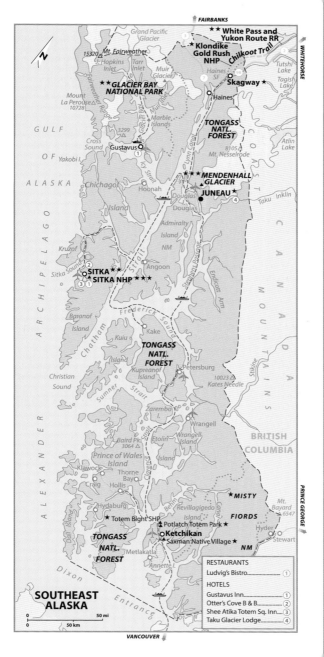

FAIRBANKS

★★ White Pass and
Yukon Route RR
★ Klondike
Gold Rush
NHP

WHITEHORSE

Grand Pacific
Glacier

15320 Mt. Fairweather

Chilkoot Trail

Tutshi
Lake

Hopkins Inlet

Tarr Inlet

Muir
Glacier

Haines SF

Skagway ★

Tagish
Lake

★★ GLACIER BAY
NATIONAL PARK

Mount
La Perouse △
10728

Marble
Islands

Haines

Atlin
Lake

GULF

3299 △

TONGASS
NATL.
FOREST

B105 △ Mt. Nesselrode

Cross
Sound

Gustavus ○

OF Yakobi I.

Icy Strait

Lynn Canal

ALASKA

Chichagof

Hoonah

★★ MENDENHALL
GLACIER
JUNEAU ★

A

R

C

H

I

P

E

L

A

G

O

Kruzof

Island

Douglas
Douglas

Taku Inklin

N

A

D

A

Admiralty
Island
NM

Taku

C

Chatham Strait

Stephens Passage

Angoon

Endicott Arm

★★ SITKA ★★
SITKA NHP ★★★

Baranof
Island

Kuiu
Island

Frederick Sound

Kake

M

O

U

N

T

A

I

N

S

Sitka Sound

Christian
Sound

TONGASS
NATL.
FOREST

Kupreanof
Island

Petersburg

10023 △
Kates Needle

Stikine

Sumner Strait

Zarembo I.

Baird Pk
3064 △

Etolin
Island

Wrangell

Wrangell
Island

Clarence Strait

BRITISH
COLUMBIA

Prince of Wales
Island

PRINCE GEORGE

Thorne
Bay

Klawock

Craig

Hollis

★ MISTY
FIORDS

Mt.
Bayard
6547 △

Hydaburg

★ Totem Bight SHP
⚓ Potlatch Totem Park ★
○ Ketchikan
★ Saxman Native Village ★

Revillagigedo
Island

Behm Canal

Hyder

Stewart

Dall Island

TONGASS
NATL.
FOREST

Metlakatla

Annette I.

NM

Dixon
Entrance

SOUTHEAST
ALASKA

RESTAURANTS	
Ludvig's Bistro	①
HOTELS	
Gustavus Inn	①
Otter's Cove B & B	②
Shee Atika Totem Sq. Inn	③
Taku Glacier Lodge	④

0   50 mi
0   50 km

VANCOUVER

SOUTHEAST ALASKA

CITIES

MUST SEE SOUTHEAST ALASKA

SKAGWAY★

96mi north of Juneau; road access from the Yukon on the Klondike Hwy. (Rte. 98) via Whitehorse 110mi northeast. Flights between Juneau and Skagway are offered by Wings of Alaska; 907-789-0790 or 800-789-9464; www.wingsof alaska.com. Main visitor center is in the historic Arctic Brotherhood Hall, on Broadway between 2nd and 3rd Aves.; open May–Sept Mon–Fri 7am–6pm, Sat–Sun 7am–5pm. 907-983-2854. www.skagway.com.

This small harbor city is best known for its historic status as the key gateway to the **Klondike gold fields** in the gold rush that began in 1897. Thousands of hopeful prospectors (hopeful gold-field suppliers) thronged here for about a decade, having shipped up from Seattle or Vancouver. Once in Skagway they traded their funds for the famous "ton of goods" that Canadian authorities required them to bring when they crossed the Yukon border at **Chilkoot Pass**, headed for the gold fields 600mi inland. The first gold reached the US in early summer 1897; by the following summer, Skagway had mushroomed to about 10,000 people. The town's main street, **Broadway**, became a thriving— and rowdy—district of saloons, gambling halls, cafes, hotels and other frontier facilities. Most famously, Jefferson "Soapy" Smith operated a saloon here until he was killed in a gunfight in 1898. Once the Klondike boom had faded, the town settled into a quiescent period as a small port (Yukon's gateway to the outside world) until the Alaska cruise industry began bringing in thousands of people in during the second half of the 20C—this time, tourists seeking Gold Rush history. Vast numbers come here for shore excursions to visit the national historic park, ride the **White Pass & Yukon Route Railroad** (see opposite), or even essay a trek across Chilkoot Pass, minus a ton of goods, of course.

The **Skagway Convention & Visitors Bureau** (*www.skagway. com*) offers a **walking tour** map of the town's historic district. Sights of special interest in the area along Broadway from First to Seventh Avenues include restored 19C wooden structures such as the **Arctic Brotherhood Hall**, with its fancy driftwood facade.

Vanishing Act

Largely dependent on now-declining resource extraction industries—timber, fisheries, mining—the area's **population** has been dropping and is predicted by state demographers to continue to do so. It's roughly 70,000, 10 percent of the state's whole. In the once-key industry, forest products, the federal government estimated that regional jobs had plummeted from 3,543 in 1990 to just 265 in 2008. Nonetheless, one industry thrives—tourism, primarily cruise ship travel.

HISTORICAL SITES

🚂 White Pass & Yukon Route Railroad★★

Depot at 231 Second Ave. $119 and up, depending on trip length. Departures early May–late Sept daily; schedules vary. 800-343-7373. www.wpyr.com.

Completed in 1900 to offer passage into the gold fields, this **narrow gauge railway** originally linked Skagway to Whitehorse, Yukon. It follows a scenic (and sometimes harrowing) route up its namesake pass. Most Skagway visitors hop aboard a morning train of restored period railcars for a half-day **excursion to the pass summit★** (*no passport required*), along which the train climbs nearly 3,000ft in 20mi, up grades as steep as 3.9 percent, through two tunnels and across numerous bridges and trestles. The jagged peaks of the coastal mountains rise on every side; waterfalls plunge into the valley as the train chugs around sharp curves. Longer itineraries are available, as far as Whitehorse, Yukon; many Skagway visitors ride the train to Whitehorse, buses to Dawson City and onward along the Alaska and Top of the World Highways into Fairbanks or Anchorage.

🚂 Klondike Gold Rush National Historical Park★

Visitor center in White Pass & Yukon Route Railroad Depot on Broadway at 2nd Ave. Open early May–late Sept daily Mon–Fri 7:30am–7pm, Sat–Sun 8am–6pm. 907-983-2921. www.nps.gov/klgo.

This park encompasses portions of Skagway's **historic district**—a dozen buildings are owned by the National Park Service—as well as the **Chilkoot Pass Trail,** up which gold-rushers struggled with their mandatory ton of supplies. Most visitors pick up a historic district map at the visitor center in the historic 1901 railway depot and stroll the town, admiring the Victorian and Edwardian boom town architecture.

The park's **museum★**, next to the park visitor center, holds an extensive array of period artifacts, from gold pans to pioneer journals. Visitors will learn the specifics of the ton of supplies gold-rushers had to haul up the 🚂 **Chilkoot Trail**—150 pounds of bacon and 400 pounds of flour, for instance. Up the street at 3rd and Broadway, the **Mascot Saloon★** (*open daily 8am–6pm*) is a historic tavern wherein photographs and small interpretive exhibits describe the hijinks that would have taken place here a century ago.

Walking up Broadway and then turning right on 5th Avenue to its end gains access to the **Moore House and Cabin,** which introduce visitors to the lives of homesteaders in the region. One can still hike the Chilkoot Trail today—as an adventurer, not a gold-seeker. The entire trail is under US or Canadian national park purview, and it's an arduous, three-day journey; permits are required and fees are charged (*up to $50 depending on the hike's length*).

SITKA★★

94 air miles southwest of Juneau; direct daily flights from Juneau and Seattle to Sitka (SIT) are provided by Alaska Airlines; www.alaskaair.com. Ferry service from Alaska Marine Highway System; www.dot.state.ak.us. Visitor center at 104 Lake St.; open May–Sept daily 8am-5pm; rest of the year Mon–Fri reduced hours. 907-747-8604 or 800-557-4852. www.sitka.org.

Alaska's first capital occupies a scenery-blessed site on the western side of Baranof Island—a relatively balmy location in which palm trees grew, for many years, on the south side of an apartment block in town. Sitkans wryly refer to their home as the "banana belt" of the state, with good reason: average annual snowfall is just 39in, and wintertime lows rarely drop below 20°F. The all-time low was 5 degrees; compare that to zero in Seattle, and –22°F in Juneau.

Not weather but ease of access, a good port and abundant sea otter population drew Russian colonizers in the late 18C, wending their way around from the Aleutian Islands. Surely they did enjoy the setting—the snowcapped summit of Mount Verstovia rises 2,550ft directly behind the town; countless islands, islets and skerries dot Sitka Sound to the south and west (buffering ocean swells); and the ice-cream cone volcanic summit of Mount Edgecumbe rises 3,202ft in the northwest distance.

Following a fierce battle in 1804 between Russian troops and Tlingit warriors, the town became the colonial capital in 1808 and grew apace through the American purchase in 1867, until Juneau supplanted it as territorial capital in 1906. Since then it has relied on fishing, trade and tourism for its relative prosperity. Sitka National Historical Park, which encompasses much of the town's historic character, was Alaska's first federal park, and celebrated its centennial in 1910. Though it's a state, rather than a federal, park, **Castle Hill,** a prominence about 100ft high which overlooks Sitka Harbor next to downtown, is an excellent vantage point for views of the town, the sound and surrounding mountains. This is the site where Russian forces built a fortress to bolster their defenses against Tlingit warriors, and where the American flag was first raised October 18, 1867. Most of the attractions below can be reached from downtown by walking.

Indian River estuary

HISTORICAL SITES

🛶 Sitka National Historical Park ★★★

Open May–Sept daily 8am–5pm.
Rest of the year Mon–Sat.
Visitor Center at the south end
of Lincoln St. 907-747-0110.
www.nps.gov/sitk.

While the history of Sitka and its
many peoples is both fascinating
and meaningful, the highlight
here is the **collection of totems**,
perhaps the finest in the US. Set
amid conifer woods at the south
end of the city, the park's **Totem
Trail★★★** (*2mi loop, easy walking*)
holds more than a dozen poles
representing the Tlingit and Haida
cultures of Southeast Alaska.
Though most of the poles are
historic, some are new, including
a 35ft commemorative pole
carved by Tlingit master Tommy
Joseph for the park's centennial
in 2010. The **visitor center**, which
incorporates the **Southeast Alaska
Indian Cultural Center**, offers
an illuminating look at the area's
Native cultures, with a longhouse,

Sitka National Historical Park
©Leslie Forsberg/Michelin

displays of ceremonial clothing
and artifacts, and an even-handed
description of the early 19C two-
year war between the Tlingits and
Russian colonists.
Separately, the mustard-yellow
1842 **Russian Bishop's House★★**
(*corner of Lincoln and Monastery
Sts.; open daily 8:30am–5pm; $4 fee
for tour*) offers a remarkable look
at not only history but pioneer
ingenuity. Park managers have

Nootka Lupine (Lupinus nootkatensis),
summer wildflower in the park

exposed portions of the house's structure to reveal the massive logs that were hand-shaped for the walls, as well as the warmth-holding foundation and insulation.

St. Michael's Cathedral★★

240 Lincoln St. Open May–Sept 9am–4pm, when cruise ships are in port. Rest of the year, call for an appointment to tour the church. 907-747-8120. www.oca.org.

When the original church edifice on this site caught fire in 1966, parishioners rushed to save, not the building, but the priceless collection of **Russian Orthodox icons★★**, illuminated books and other religious artifacts within. Remarkably, the entire inventory survived. On display now in the reconstructed cathedral are gold-painted and gilded portraits of saints, prayer books, crosses, ecclesiastical garments and artifacts constituting perhaps the finest such collection in North America. The "Sitka Mother of God,"

Yup'ik Eskimo mask, collected at St. Michael Alaska 1892, Sheldon Jackson Museum

©Barry McWayne, Sheldon Jackson Museum II-G-11

icon is reputed to effect miracles. Though the building reflects the classic Orthodox style of the 1848 original, it dates, of course, to its reconstruction in 1966.

Sheldon Jackson Museum★

104 College Dr. Open mid-May–mid-Sept daily 9am–5pm. Rest of the year Tue–Sat 10am–4pm. $5. 907-747-8981. museums.alaska.gov.

This museum is the oldest museum in the state. Three distinctions make this facility stand out: it was the first concrete structure in Alaska when built in 1897. Its octagonal shape was unusual then and remains so now. Most importantly, it holds one of the state's largest collections of **Alaska Native artifacts**, gathered largely by Rev. Sheldon Jackson, a Presbyterian missionary who founded the museum. One of his purposes in establishing it was to provide insight into the lives of Alaska Natives' ancestors. Highlights of the nearly 5,500 artifacts amassed from all of Alaska's major cultural groups include an Athabascan birchbark canoe; an Aleut seal-skin kayak called a baidarka; Haida carvings made of argillite, the black stone found on Haida Gwaii off British Columbia; and a vast number of **Eskimo masks★**, baskets, ivory carvings and garments. In summer *(mid-May–mid-Sept)*, visitors might have an opportunity to watch Native artists from across Alaska demonstrate their skills such as weaving, carving and beadworking.

FOR FUN

Alaska Raptor Center ★★

1000 Raptor Way (south edge of town). Open May–Sept daily 8am–4pm. Rest of the year, call for opening times. $12. 907-747-8662. www.alaskaraptor.org.

The main residents here are injured **bald eagles**. They have been brought to the center for rehabilitation or, in the case of recovery insufficient to return to nature, permanent residence. Alas, many eagles are still shot by lawbreakers, or otherwise harmed—some 100-200 birds are brought here each year. Owls, ospreys, hawks and other birds of prey all live or rehabilitate at the center. Most visitors come to meet one of the resident eagles; staff members bring them out for "up close and personal" demonstrations of their implacable, predatory gaze. "Volta" is often the day's star. "Raptors-in-residence" live in large pens or netted, forest enclosures, and trainers occasionally take the birds out for "walks" along the adjacent Indian River.

Fortress of the Bear

4639 Sawmill Creek Rd. Open May–Sept daily 9am–6pm. Winter Fri-Sun 10am–4pm. $10. 907-747-3032. www.fortressofthebear.org.

Opened in 2009, this nascent facility aspires to become a caregiver like the Raptor Center on the other side of Sitka—a place where animals, in this case ursines, can find refuge if they are no longer able to live in the wild. Largely populated with orphan coastal **brown bear** cubs, the haven occasionally has **black bears** in residence as well. Meanwhile, visitors have an opportunity to see, learn about and support the bears. The facility serves as a place city residents and food handlers such as restaurants can "recycle" food waste—into the bears' bellies.

Sitka Sound Science Center

834 Lincoln St. Open in summer 8am–5pm on cruise ship days. Winter Mon–Fri 10am–3pm. $5. 907-747-8878. www.sitka sitkascience.org.

Bald eagle in flight

© Todd Harless/U.S. Fish and Wildlife Service

FOR FUN

Though primarily a research center, this downtown facility features an **aquarium** whose display tanks and touch tanks focus on the marine species of Sitka Sound, from small bivalves to orcas—the last in the form of a killer whale skeleton newly installed.

The 800-gallon **"Wall of Water"** is the highlight.

Visitors are also welcome to stroll the grounds of the **fish hatchery** that is part of the center.

PERFORMING ARTS

🦁 New Archangel Dancers★★

Performances are usually held at Harrigan Centennial Hall, 330 Harbor Dr. $10. 907-747-5516. www.newarchangeldancers.com. Though called "Sitka" by most (a corruption of the Tlingit phrase *shee atika*), the town was actually named New Archangel by the Russians. The resident **New Archangel Dancers** reflect this history in a most intriguing way— the troupe is composed entirely of local, non-professional female dancers because when it started in 1969, no men were interested. Dancers perform Russian classics such as the "Cossack horsemen's dance," and 35 other dances from Russia, Ukraine, Moldova and allied areas. The colorful costumes and vigorous performances offer a memorable nod to Sitka's Russian heritage—though none of the dancers themselves are of Russian lineage.

🦁 Sheet'ka Kwaan Naa Kahidi Native Dancers

204 Katlian St. Performances are held mid-day or mid-afternoon five days a week in summer, usually on ship-call days; call for times. $10. 907-747-7290; www.sitkatours.com. Tlingit ceremonial dances, chants and song are performed by these dancers in a traditional clan house.

New Archangel Dancers

©Leslie Forsberg/Michelni

Ketchikan's Creek Street

©Leslie Forsberg/Michelin

CITIES

KETCHIKAN

230 air miles south of Juneau; direct daily service from Juneau and Seattle to Ketchikan (KTN) is provided by Alaska Airlines; www.alaskaair.com. Ferry service is provided by Alaska Marine Highway System; www.dot.state. ak.us. Visitor center on the waterfront at Front and Main Sts; open May–Sept daily 8am–5pm; rest of the year Mon–Fri 8am–5pm. 907-225-6166 or 800-770-3300. www.visit-ketchikan.com.

One of the three mainstay towns for cruise ship calls (along with Juneau and Sitka), Ketchikan can at first be disconcerting for thoughtful travelers—downtown's wharf-side Front Street is lined with a plethora of tourist shops selling, improbably, diamonds and other gems *(see sidebar p63)*. One must get past this entry to find the worthy attractions the city offers visitors.

Just up from the waterfront lies the highly touted, but rather tawdry **Creek Street Historic District**.

A reconstructed boardwalk from Ketchikan's rowdy boom days in the early 20C is lined with souvenir shops, taverns and costumed role players purporting to represent brothel owners and inebriated prospectors. They are reflecting actual history—this area was a famous red-light district shut down in 1953. Today, its shops concentrate on tourist trinkets such as scented soap and Pendleton blankets. Aside from the Creek Street district, the **Southeast Alaska Discovery Center** *(see The Great Outdoors below)* and the City Museum, which are easily reached by walking from downtown, most of the city's sights require vehicle transport of some kind; taxis are numerous. For transportation to and narrated tours of the three totem sites outside downtown— Totem Bight, Saxman and Potlatch Parks *(see below)*— contact **Northern Tours of Alaska** *(tours $40-$49; 907-247-6457 or 877-461-8687).*

TOTEM SITES

⚓ Totem Heritage Center★★

601 Deermount St. Open May–Sept daily 8am–5pm. Rest of the year Mon–Fri 1pm–5pm. $5. 907-225-5900. ktn-ak.us.

The many treasures on display in this superb small museum (essentially, it's the city's history museum) include more than 40 historic **Haida and Tlingit totems★★** "rescued" from abandoned villages throughout Southeast Alaska in 1970. Poles are shown as they were found, rather than retouched or restored, to honor the traditional principle that totems are meant to return to the ground eventually—although many are preserved in climate-controlled cases. Baskets, hats and other artifacts are also on exhibit. An active **carving center** often has modern carvers teaching and learning traditional arts.

⚓ Potlatch Totem Park★

9809 Totem Bight Rd., 10mi north of Ketchikan along North Tongass Hwy. Open May-Sept daily 8am-5pm. Winter limited hours. 907-225-4445. www.potlatchpark.com.

Adjacent to Totem Bight State Park, this attraction differs from it chiefly in that its carvings are new, and its active art-creation enterprise relies on the tourist trade to support local artists. A newly constructed **bighouse** holds dioramas and carvings representing all the major Native cultures of the region, as do several totems on-site. **Tribal houses** and a **classic car collection** are also on display.

Saxman Native Village

©Leslie Forsberg/Michelin

⚓ Saxman Native Village★

3mi south of downtown Ketchikan on South Tongass Hwy. Open May–Sept daily 8am–6pm. $5 totem park admission. 907-225-4846. www.capefoxtours.com.

It's true that this village is an unabashed tourist attraction—buses carrying cruise-ship passengers fill the parking lot all summer, and independent travelers should first call to arrange a visit during show times. It is, nonetheless, an excellent, heart-felt exhibition of Tlingit life, arts and culture. Visitors are invited to tour the **Beaver Clan bighouse** and nearby carving shed, and watch a marvelous performance (*additional $24 fee*) of traditional song, chant, storytelling and dance by the ⚓ **Cape Fox Dancers★★**—typically, performers range from kids younger than 10 to seniors in their 8th decade, just as would have been true two centuries ago.

The surrounding village holds one of the largest collections of totems in the US; of particular note is the "**Seward Shame Pole**," on which the red-faced depiction of William Seward recalls his discourtesy to

SOUTHEAST ALASKA

MUST DO

the Tlingit people a century and a half ago. When Seward toured Alaska to see what he had bought, the Saxman villagers feted him with a great potlatch celebration. But Seward failed to invite them to his village—Washington, DC—in return. For shame!

Totem Bight State Historical Park★

10mi north of Ketchikan on North Tongass Hwy. 907-247-8574. dnr.alaska.gov/parks/units/totembgh.htm.
Created during the Great Depression by the Civilian Conservation Corps as one of Ketchikan's early visitor attractions—and an attempt to preserve the art of Native carving—this lovely park (now owned by the state) holds a replica clan house and 14 totems. The totems are largely duplicates of older ones that Forest Service officials found on the site in 1938, when village construction began. Notable are the house posts on the bighouse, which feature a clan leader, adorned by a spruce-root hat, ready for a potlatch. The 14 poles include both Haida and Tlingit designs, such as a **Wandering Raven House Entrance Pole★**, the entry hole in which was designed to be easily barred during battles.

The Meaning of Totem Poles

Instantly recognized worldwide as symbols of North Pacific indigenous culture, the hand-carved totem poles that once stood along the shores of Native Alaskan coastal villages were both spiritual and practical works of art. The designs honored the natural spirits the people relied on, from Raven to Salmon, Whale and Bear. Poles also announced clan lineages and carried other social messages—such as the famous Seward Shame Pole in Saxman, near Ketchikan, which scoffs at William Seward's discourtesy.

Almost always carved from rot-resistant Western red-cedar or Alaska yellow-cedar (neither of which is actually a "cedar" species), a pole took months or years to create. Raising one was, and is, a ceremonial occasion of great importance, accompanied by a potlatch gathering and feast such as that which greeted the raising of the Centennial Pole at Sitka National Historical Park in 2010.

Large numbers of historic poles were amassed by collectors—often illegally or unethically—in the 19C and early 20C throughout the Pacific Northwest. Many of them wound up in museums as far away as Europe and Asia, where their display was improper in two ways: totems are meant as semi-sacred objects for the villages and clans that raised them; and they are traditionally supposed to decay with age, returning to nature from whence they came. New totems carved by new generations continue the cycle of life.

The world's largest totem is a 173ft, two-section pole in Canada's Alert Bay, British Columbia. But sheer height is far from the only attribute to measure as you gaze upon these wonders, new or old. They are literally the stories of rich and thriving cultures, told in form and color graven in wood.

TOTEM SITES

THE GREAT OUTDOORS

Misty Fiords National Monument★

40mi east of Ketchikan; boat or floatplane access only. Visitor center is the Southeast Alaska Discovery Center in Ketchikan (see below). 907-228-6220. www.fs.fed.us/r10/tongass.

Yet another of Alaska's wild preserves that is unreachable by road, Misty Fiords encompasses almost 3 million acres of fjord, forest, mountain and water that is completely wilderness, save a small mineral rights reserve. Here, granite escarpments rise thousands of feet above still ocean inlets, waterfalls pour from the heights, loons call and bears prowl the underbrush.

The towering cliffs that line many of the fjords are often likened to the landscape of Yosemite; fog, drizzle and mist are indeed almost daily occurrences. Most visitors arrive on cruise ships, or private boat charter from Ketchikan, or

New Eddystone Rock, Misty Fiords National Monument

Used by permission, U.S. Forest Service

floatplane, also from Ketchikan. The downtown Ketchikan **Southeast Alaska Discovery Center** *(50 Main St.; open summer Mon–Fri 8am–4pm, winter Fri noon–8pm; 907-228-6220; www.*

Nooya Lake, Misty Fiords National Monument

Used by permission, U.S. Forest Service

Not Your Best Friend

First-time visitors to Ketchikan, Juneau and to a lesser extent, Sitka and other Southeast towns, are surprised to find an inordinate number of diamond, gem and jewelry stores along downtown streets. Is there some home-grown jewelry industry behind this? Not really; there is virtually no gem production in Alaska, and gold mining is largely confined to the western and interior parts of the state, excepting a new mine north of Juneau. (A trivia fact that invariably amazes people is that Nevada—not Alaska—leads the US in gold production, by far.)

The retail gem parade in Southeast tourist towns is a classic example of the laws of supply and demand—in this case, a ready supply of customers in the form of thousands who step off cruise ships every day four months a year. Virtually none of these stores are open year-round; most are staffed by non-residents; the wares within almost all originate far away, including Africa, South America and Asia. In other words, the benefit to local economies is modest.

The quality and pricing are no better than run-of-the-mill jewelry stores in the Lower 48, and the sophistication level is likewise: ask the salesclerks if they offer conflict-free diamonds (such as those from Canada) and they will profess to have no idea what you mean.

Thoughtful Southeast Alaska visitors looking for souvenirs of their journey will be well advised to focus on regionally authentic items, such as smoked salmon, woodcrafts and Alaska Native art.

---

alaskacenters.gov/ketchikan.cfm) serves as the information clearinghouse for National Forest, National Monument and State of Alaska preserves and properties in the region. It is also a fine **interpretive center** describing the area's biologically rich ecosystem. Exhibits illustrate the life cycle of Pacific anadromous salmon, the delicate balance between forest, water and fish, and the lifestyles of the indigenous people who both relied on and honored their natural surroundings.

A high-definition **movie★** created especially for the center (*$5 admission*) documents the ecosystem of the Tongass forest that embraces 16.8 million acres and is located just outside of town limits.

Tongass National Forest

For guides, outfitting and transportation information, consult the Southeast Alaska Discovery Center (see above). 907-228-6220.
www.fs.fed.us/r10/tongass.

Ketchikan sits in the heart of Tongass, America's largest national forest, at 17 million acres, and serves as one of the main visitor access points. This empire of wood and water is the home of countless islands and inlets, lakes and streams. Ancient Sitka spruce trees reach past 200ft; bears prowl the woods and waters where humans are only visitors. The national forest maintains more than 100 cabins and reservable shelters (www. recreation.gov) for wilderness travelers.

THE GREAT OUTDOORS

ANCHORAGE★

Holding nearly half the state's residents, Alaska's largest metropolitan area (population 380,000) occupies the south-central part of the state. The city and borough of Anchorage encompass a vast rectangle stretching nearly 50mi north to south, and 20mi from the Cook Inlet waterfront on the west to the eastern alpine heights of the Chugach Range. The city is so large that one of its "neighborhoods," Girdwood, lies 45min from downtown via high-speed highway.

Starting out as a tent city for pioneers and rail workers in 1914, Anchorage sprouted into a **frontier town**. Fort Richardson and Elmendorf Air Force Base helped expand the population to more than 30,000 by 1950. A devastating **earthquake** struck the city in 1964: at 9.2 magnitude, it was the second largest quake in recorded world history. Afterwards, the city was reinvigorated by new buildings as well as the development of oil in **Prudhoe Bay**. A transportation center, Anchorage is linked to other parts of the state by air, by the Seward and Glenn highways, and by rail. Anchorage's airport is an **international hub** for commercial shipping; dozens of jumbo jets stop here between Asia and Europe. The city boasts an extensive recreational **trail network**: 135 miles of paved off-street path and 300 miles unpaved. This huge land area (almost 2,000sq mi) contains thousands of acres of **mountain wilderness**, and the extensive Anchorage recreation/greenbelt system brings the wilderness into the city. Moose are a common sight, especially in winter; bears are occasionally seen. Lakes and hiking trails and quiet forests are inside the city limits. Glaciers plow down from the windswept peaks of the Chugach; tumbling streams pass through birch-lined valleys where beavers build massive dams. Anglers gather by downtown's **Ship Creek** for a salmon run each summer. Cosmopolitan **advantages** here range from superb restaurants and lively theaters to fine bookstores and art galleries, and well, four-lane freeways. Popular nightclub venues attract performers from "outside." The city is coffee-mad—more so than Seattle or Portland—and local roasters and espresso vendors are endemic. Anchorage is also extraordinarily multicultural: city neighborhood Mountain View is the most ethnically diverse census tract in the entire US.

Fast Facts

Land area: 1,961sq mi (5,079 sq km), bigger than Rhode Island

Population: 295,000 in the city (41 percent of Alaska's population); 380,000 metro area

Languages spoken by residents: more than 90

Average annual precipitation: 16 inches

Average annual snowfall: 75 inches

Daylight: midsummer 22hrs; midwinter 5½ hrs

Practical Information

When to Go

Heavy snow is rare, and sunny weather often arrives in March and April—which can be among the best times to visit. May and June are usually delightful, whereas the weather deteriorates in mid-August.

Getting There

✦ **By Air – Ted Stevens Anchorage International Airport** (ANC) (*907-266-2526; www.anchorageairport.com*) lies 6mi southwest of downtown. Alaska Airlines (*800-252-7522; www.alaskaair.com*) has flights between Anchorage and Seattle almost hourly, daily service to Portland, and seasonal service to Los Angeles, Denver and Chicago. Other airlines serving Anchorage include United, JetBlue, Delta and American. In-state airlines include **Ravn** (*907-266-8394; flyravn.com*) and **Pen Airways** (*907-771-2640; www.penair.com),* which fly between Anchorage and Homer, Valdez and Kodiak.

✦ **By Ferry** – Service from Bellingham WA from **Alaska Marine Highway System** (*www.dot.state.ak.us/amhs*), whose nearest ports of call to Anchorage are Seward and Whittier.

✦ **By Car** – Anchorage can be reached by driving the Alaska Highway through Canada to Tok Junction, then turning south on the Glenn Highway (Rte. 1). The journey is 1,575mi (5 days) from the Alaska Highway start in Dawson Creek, British Columbia; and 1,868mi (7 days) from Seattle, via the Cassiar Highway through British Columbia.

Getting Around

✦ **By Car – Rental cars** are available at Anchorage airport from all major companies. Passenger cars are adequate for the region, even during winter months, as highway crews keep main roads cleared well.

✦ **By Bus** – Bus service between Anchorage, Fairbanks and Whitehorse (Yukon Territory) from **Interior Alaska Bus Line** (*907-277-6652 or 800-770-6652; interioralaskabusline.com*). Bus service in Anchorage is modest: the city's **People Mover** is more for commuters; www.muni.org. Some outlying attractions, such as the Alaska Zoo and Alaska Native Heritage Center, offer **free shuttles** from downtown in summer.

✦ **By Train – Alaska Railroad** (*907-265- 2494 or 800-544-0552; www.alaskarailroad.com*) links Anchorage, Seward, Denali National Park and Fairbanks.

Visitor Information

4th Ave. & F St.; Jun–Aug daily 8am–7pm, early Sept and late May 8am–6pm, winter 9am–4pm; 907-257-2363. At airport's baggage claim: 907-266-2437. www.anchorage.net.

MUSEUMS

Anchorage Museum★★★

625 C St. Open May–Sept daily 9am–6pm. Rest of year Tue–Sat 10am–6pm Sun noon–6pm. $12. 907-929-9200. www.anchoragemuseum.org.

Doubled in size in 2010 (and expanding in 2017), this premier museum is devoted to Arctic and sub-Arctic culture. Among its many highlights is the **Smithsonian Arctic Studies Center★★★**, which brought to Alaska priceless treasures of indigenous Alaska arts and crafts that had been stored for decades in Washington, DC. Among the hundreds of items on display, treasures range from a 19C Tlingit war helmet to evocative ceremonial masks to carefully wrought gut parkas whose beauty belies their practical value. Fascinating videos recount the traditions and modern lives of Alaska's many Native peoples. The hall illustrates the close connection between aboriginal Alaskans and their cousins in Siberia. Several massive **Sydney Laurence canvases** include Alaska's most famous artist's equally famous depictions of Denali. An expansive **Alaska History Gallery★** provides a thorough but concise review of the state's story from Russian colonization to oil development. Excellent temporary exhibits focus on the changing lands and cultures of the Arctic world.

The museum's **Muse** cafe focuses on seafood dishes such as crab cakes and halibut burgers.

Alaska Native Heritage Center★★★

East of downtown. 8800 Heritage Center Dr. Open mid-May–Labor Day daily 9am–5pm. $25. 907-330-8000. www.alaskanative.net. Free shuttle from downtown.

Occupying a pastoral 26-acre site flanking a picturesque small lake, this expansive facility allows visitors to learn about Alaska's 11 major indigenous cultural groups, ranging from the well-known Inuit to the little-known Alutiiq. The **Hall of Cultures★** holds an

Smithsonian Arctic Studies Center, Anchorage Museum

Courtesy of the Anchorage Museum

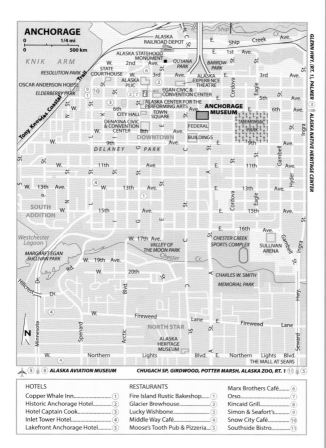

KNIK   ARM

RESOLUTION PARK
OSCAR ANDERSON HOUSE
ELDERBERRY PARK

Tony Knowles Coastal Trail

ALASKA RAILROAD DEPOT
E. Ship Creek Cr. Ave.
W. 2nd Ave.
ALASKA STATEHOOD MONUMENT
QUYANA PARK
W. STATE COURTHOUSE
W. 3rd Ave.
ALASKA PLIC
ALASKA EXPERIENCE THEATRE
EGAN CIVIC & CONVENTION CENTER
ALASKA CENTER FOR THE PERFORMING ARTS
CITY HALL
TOWN SQUARE
DENAINA CIVIC & CONVENTION CENTER
W. 6th Ave.
W. 8th Ave.
DOWNTOWN
W. 9th Ave.
ANCHORAGE MUSEUM
FEDERAL BUILDINGS
E. 1st Ave.
Ship Creek
BARROW PARK
E. 3rd Ave.
Cordova St.
Eagle St.
E. 5th Ave.
E. 6th Ave.
DELANEY PARK
E. 9th Ave.
MEMORIAL PARK
Ingra St.

W. 11th Ave. / E. 11th Ave.
SOUTH ADDITION
W. 13th Ave. / E. 13th Ave.
W. 15th Ave. / E. 15th Ave.
Cordova St.
Eagle St.
Gambell St.
Hyder St.

Westchester Lagoon
MARGARET EAGAN SULLIVAN PARK
W. 17th Ave.
VALLEY OF THE MOON PARK
Chester Cr.
E. 16th Ave.
CHESTER CREEK SPORTS COMPLEX
SULLIVAN ARENA
Gambell St.
Ingra Hwy.

Hillcrest Dr.
W. 19th Ave.
W. 20th
Blvd.
CHARLES W. SMITH MEMORIAL PARK

Minnesota Dr.
Spenard
Arctic Blvd.
W. Fireweed Lane
NORTH STAR
ALASKA HERITAGE MUSEUM
W. Northern Lights Blvd.
E. Fireweed Lane
E. Northern Lights Blvd.
THE MALL AT SEARS
Seward Hwy.

N

✈ ⑤ ⑧ ALASKA AVIATION MUSEUM   CHUGACH SP, GIRDWOOD, POTTER MARSH, ALASKA ZOO, RT. 1 ⑪ ⑤

HOTELS	RESTAURANTS	
Copper Whale Inn ①	Fire Island Rustic Bakeshop ①	Marx Brothers Café ⑥
Historic Anchorage Hotel ②	Glacier Brewhouse ②	Orso ⑦
Hotel Captain Cook ③	Lucky Wishbone ③	Kincaid Grill ⑧
Inlet Tower Hotel ④	Middle Way Café ④	Simon & Seafort's ⑨
Lakefront Anchorage Hotel ⑤	Moose's Tooth Pub & Pizzeria ⑤	Snow City Café ⑩
		Southside Bistro ⑪

indoor collection of interactive exhibits documenting the historic lifestyles and modern realities of the Great Land's Native peoples, with a wealth of items from historic baskets to modern art. In the same building, the 🏛 **Gathering Place** is a staging venue for Native dance, chant, song, story-telling and other performances.

Outside, six life-size reconstructed **traditional dwellings** illustrate how indigenous peoples lived.

Walking the path around the lake and through the woods, visitors can explore a Haida longhouse, an Inupiaq sod house and other structures. Costumed interpreters representing the different cultures are often on hand to answer questions, such as How did cultures living in treeless areas find timbers for their houses? (drift logs). A massive collection of **whalebones** abuts the Inuit display.

Floatplanes at Lake Hood

© Roy Neese/Visit Anchorage

artwork. And, in a new activity, past Iditarod champion John Baker (2011 winner), an Inupiat from Kotzebue, offers wheeled **dogsled rides** throughout the summer.

Alaska Aviation Museum★

4721 Aircraft Dr., at south side of Lake Hood. Open mid-May–mid-Sept daily 9am–5pm. Rest of the year Wed–Sat 9am–5pm, Sun noon–5pm. $15. 907-248-5325. www.alaskaairmuseum.org.

Few places are as reliant on aviation, both commercial and private, as Alaska—much of the state is not reachable by any road (including the capital, Juneau). Dedicated to that affinity, this museum includes indoor exhibits on famous aircraft, airlines and pilots that have served Alaska over a century. Notable are the **Curtis J-1 Standard**, in which legendary airman Noel Wien made the first flight from Anchorage to Fairbanks in 1924; and a **Grumman Super Widgeon** amphibious plane from 1943. There's even a cockpit where visitors sit behind the controls.

The center's gift shop is one of the best places in the city to acquire authentic Native crafts and

---

Anchorage: Uniquely Yours

Cosmopolitan though their city may be, Anchorage residents relish jokes like "You know you're in Alaska when the parish fundraiser is sausage making, not bingo." Indeed, many Anchorage freezers are filled with moose meat each fall, and reindeer sausage substitutes for hot dogs at downtown street food stands.

Alaskans are quite aware of the outside world, but cherish their own unique identity. The best example may be what Anchorage residents conceived as a new event in the annual Fur Rendezvous winter festival. It's their answer to the famous running of the bulls in Pamplona, Spain. The "Running of the Reindeer" is Fur Rondy's most popular event (*see Calendar of Events*). The event epitomizes Anchorage, the only city where you may be having a world-class gourmet dinner at a white linen restaurant—but you never know when a moose might stroll by outside to browse the shrubbery.

Outside on the grounds are more airplanes of historical significance. Aircraft restoration is ongoing here; visitors may ask to watch the process.

Next door, the **Lake Hood seaplane base**—busiest in the world, with 190 planes arriving or departing daily—offers an opportunity to watch Alaska aviation in action. The din of seaplanes taking off and landing on the lake adds realism to the impressive compendium of the state's aviation history.

Alaska Museum of Science and Nature

About 2mi east of downtown. 201 N. Bragaw St. 907-274-2400. Open year-round Mon–Sat 10am–5pm. $5. www.alaskamuseum.org.

The key attraction at this modest facility is a collection of mammal bones, including skulls ranging from modern-day wolves to a prehistoric panther, now extinct. Visitors are welcome to touch samples in the collection of Alaska rocks and minerals, the largest in the state.

THE GREAT OUTDOORS

Chugach State Park★★

East of downtown. Numerous entrances, including Eagle River, Hillside, Eklutna and McHugh Creek. Open year-round daily. $5 day-use parking fee. 907-269-8400. dnr.alaska.gov/parks.

The crown jewel of the Alaska state parks system, this vast preserve of 495,204 acres—third-largest state park in the US—encompasses most of the eastern two-thirds of the borough of Anchorage. It harbors immense stretches of wilderness, from alpine tundra above timberline to subalpine lake to lowland birch, cottonwood and spruce forest. Wilderness trekking, skiing and camping are common activities, though only for expert wilderness travelers. Day hiking, bike riding and wildlife-watching are excellent choices in the park. Virtually all Anchorage visitors experience the park, at least visually, as it forms the entire mountain skyline east of the city.

Hiking trails into the park depart numerous trailheads throughout Anchorage, ranging from Girdwood to Eagle River. Particularly popular is the **Flattop Mountain Trail**, a steep but fairly short (1.5 mi) scramble up to a spectacular viewpoint; it departs from Glen Alps trailhead, at the terminus of Glen Alps Road in south Anchorage.

Several day-use areas along Turnagain Arm, south of Anchorage, are within the park: **McHugh Creek Picnic area** (*mile 112, Seward Highway*), and **Beluga Point** (*mile 110.5, Seward Highway*), from which the point's namesake whales are sometimes seen.

A separate facility, but within the park, **Eagle River Nature Center** (*32750 Eagle River Rd.; open May–Sept Wed–Sun 10am–5pm; rest of the year Fri–Sun; $5 parking; 907-694-2108; www.ernc.org*) features compact exhibits on the park's natural environment. Especially popular are the pelts of beaver, fox, lynx and other indigenous animals available to touch.

Hiking trails from here wind through riparian woods in the river valley; moose and bears are common sights.

Kincaid Park★★

Encompassing a broad headland overlooking Cook Inlet southwest of Anchorage International Airport, this 1,400-acre park is the terminus of the Tony Knowles Coastal Trail. Here bicycle riders, walkers, skiers and skaters who have come all the way from downtown reach the end of **Planet Walk**, with Pluto at the 10.3mi end point. Each step on the trail, from its beginning downtown at 5th Avenue and G Street, metaphorically represents the distance light travels in one second through the solar system.

The **panorama★★** from the park's highest point encompasses Cook Inlet, Turnagain Arm, the mountains of the Kenai Peninsula, Mount Susitna across Cook Inlet, and on clear days, Denali far to the northwest.

Tony Knowles Coastal Trail★★

Access near Alaska Railroad depot at the west end of West 5th Ave. downtown. 907-343-7529. www.muni.org.

Named for an Alaska governor and former Anchorage mayor who vigorously promoted public lands conservation, this splendid paved trail winds along the Cook Inlet shoreline for 10.2mi.

Along the way it passes through or beside quiet neighborhoods, Westchester Lagoon *(below)*, birch forests, Earthquake Park *(opposite)* and other greenbelts. It finishes by winding up to the viewpoint at Kincaid Park.

Moose are often seen; bird-watching is excellent; wildflowers abound from June to late September. It's one of the most enchanting urban recreation trails in North America.

Bike rentals are available downtown at **Copper Whale Inn** (*West 5th and L St.; www. copperwhale.com*) and **Downtown Bicycle Rentals** on 4th Avenue (*www.alaska-bike-rentals.com*).

Tony Knowles Coastal Trail

© Cathryn Posey/Visit Anchorage

Alaska Zoo★

South of downtown. 4731 O'Malley Rd. 907-346-2133. Open Jun–Aug daily 9am–9pm. Rest of the year hours vary. $12. www.alaskazoo. org. Free shuttle from downtown visitor center hourly mid-May–mid-Sept.

While not a major zoo by Lower 48 standards, this engaging facility near the Chugach foothills affords an opportunity to see Alaska wild animals such as musk-ox, moose, porcupines, Dall sheep and wolves as well as other Arctic and sub-arctic creatures from around the world. Highlights include rare Amur tigers, snow leopards, wolverines and other animals even seasoned wilderness travelers are unlikely to see in the wild.

Earthquake Park★

5101 Point Woronzof Dr. 907-343-7529. www.muni.org.
The shoreline landscape here, bisected by the Tony Knowles Trail, offers a compelling visual reminder of the 9.2-Richter-scale earthquake that devastated Anchorage in 1964. The ground is folded in ripples, some almost 5ft high, as if it were a massive rumpled quilt, evidencing the monumental displacement from the quake. Here, along the shore, subsidence dropped this piece of land.

Potter Marsh Bird Sanctuary★

Seward Hwy. Parking area entrance is just south of the highway's Rabbit Creek exit. www.adfg.alaska.gov.
This refuge occupies a vast wetland along the Seward Highway, just south of the main section of Anchorage. Its position next to Turnagain Arm means it is invariably populated by migratory waterfowl such as trumpeter swans, Arctic terns, and innumerable ducks, and raptors such as the beautiful northern harrier. A 1,550ft boardwalk takes visitors out into the marsh; the bordering willow brush means moose are often seen, and salmon migrate into Rabbit Creek July through October.

Swans at Potter Marsh Bird Sanctuary

©Karen Laubenstein/U.S. Fish and Wildlife Service

THE GREAT OUTDOORS

Neither Rain nor Snow

Wintertime Anchorage visitors will see a sight that strikes residents of more temperate climes as, well, bizarre—heavily clad bicycle riders, wending their way along city trails and streets on bikes equipped with studded snow tires and special gloved handles, even though it may be zero degrees and the streets are clogged with snow and ice. Avid riders here don't care to abandon their bikes just because winter has arrived, and so hundreds simply keep riding, either for recreation on the city's trails network, or for travel to work. More than 300 bicycle commuters commute year-round in Anchorage, and local recreation enthusiasts believe the phenomenon began here.

🚣 Westchester Lagoon★
At the end of West 15th Ave.
907-343-7529. www.muni.org.
A lovely wetland preserve just a bit southwest of downtown Anchorage, the lagoon anchors the shoreline end of the Chester Creek greenbelt trail.

Ospreys, eagles, ducks, loons and geese are common summer sights. Hiking trails encircle both parts of the lagoon, which is bisected by Spenard Avenue. In summer, kayaking and canoeing are excellent ways to enjoy the lagoon; in winter, part of the surface is kept free of snow to serve as an outdoor 🛷 **ice skating** rink. Canoe, kayak and skate rentals are available through various outdoor outfitters in the city nearby.

🏌 Anchorage Golf Course
3651 O'Malley Rd. $63/round.
Open late Apr–mid-Oct daily, depending on spring and fall weather. 907-522-3363.
Golf in Alaska offers both amateur and expert golfers several unique facets—chief among them the opportunity to play the famous "midnight golf" in the period around midsummer. Golfers also frequently see moose, eagles, porcupines and occasionally bears; special "local rules" govern those encounters, such as when a moose steals your ball. (Yes, it happens.) Anchorage's main course open to the public wanders a ridge overlooking the city; the links have plenty to challenge experienced golfers yet the course is friendly to beginners. It sports occasional course features that are unique to Alaska, like permafrost slumps (permafrost is ground whose temperature stays below 32°F year-round) and glacial erratics—huge boulders left behind by retreating glaciers that serve as very effective course hazards.

SHOPPING

🦫 **David Green Master Furrier**
Showroom at B St. and 4th Ave.
907-277-9595.
www.davidgreenfurs.com.
Anchorage's best-regarded fur garment-maker and retailer, family-owned, has been in operation for more than 80 years. Relying largely on Alaska furs such as beaver, fox and mink, the garments are exquisite (and expensive) samples of the furrier's art.

Market & Festival
Between C and E Sts., at 3rd Ave.
Mid-May–mid-Sept Sat–Sun
10am–6pm. www.anchorage
markets.com.
Downtown Anchorage's weekly summer market has many booths in which local crafters offer handmade goods. Distinctive items include birch syrup, jewelry carved from fossil mammoth tusks, and handmade fur garments. Market regulations govern the origin of items sold here.

Oomingmak Store
604 H St. 907-272-9225.
www.qiviut.com.
This wholly authentic cooperative offers the wares of Native women, living in remote villages, who handknit superb garments, blankets and other fiber-works. *Qiviut* is the fine undercoat hair that musk-ox shed each spring; it's gathered by hand and spun, like sheep's wool.

🦫 **Title Wave Books**
1360 W. Northern Lights Blvd. 907-278-9283. www.wavebooks.com.
Just south of downtown, this

🦫 **Native Arts and Crafts**
Buying Native arts and crafts is tricky. Many trinkets, carvings and souvenirs sold in tourist-oriented Anchorage stores may appear to be of Native origin, especially totems, masks and supposed Eskimo carvings—yet are actually manufactured in Asia.

The best places to buy real Native art are the 🦫 **Alaska Native Heritage Center** and the 🦫 **gift shop at the Alaska Native Medical Center** in downtown Anchorage *(4315 Diplomacy Dr.; 907-563-2662; anmc.org)*. Both these nonprofit organizations promote support for Native culture. Genuine Native art often features a "Silver Hand" emblem.

massive store is the premier Alaska bookstore, offering hundreds of titles by Alaska authors on Alaska subjects. Used and new volumes.

Ulu Factory
211 W. Ship Creek Ave. 907-276-3119; theulufactory.com.
Above all else, Anchorage visitors seek Native art, and Northlands remembrances like a "ulu knife," a bone- or wood-handled device with a semicircular blade, originally used by Arctic peoples for fleshing whale carcasses, seal skins and such. Tourists don't need a tool for that; nonetheless hordes of visitors flock to this factory to buy one to take home. *Please remember ulu knives cannot be packed into carry-on luggage for flights home—TSA officials at Anchorage International seize dozens a week.*

EXCURSIONS

Girdwood

38mi south of downtown along Rte. 1, the Seward Hwy. (about a 1hr drive). Alaska Railroad has scheduled service between Anchorage and Girdwood, May–Sept; alaksarailroad.com.

This Anchorage "neighborhood" lies within the municipal limits, yet it is a wholly separate and distinct enclave, with about 2,300 residents, sitting in a valley abutting Turnagain Arm. It is best known as the home of Alyeska Ski Resort, whose tram (*see opposite*) carries skiers and nonskiers alike to a dizzying pinnacle with sensational views of **Turnagain Arm** and the Kenai Peninsula beyond. Hiking trails lead into the nearby temperate rain forest— perhaps the northernmost in North America. At the foot of the ski resort, **The Bake Shop** (*Olympic Circle; open year-round daily 7am–7pm; 907-783-2831*) is famed far and wide for its aromatic cinnamon rolls.

Alyeska Resort★★

1000 Arlberg Ave., at the Alyeska Hotel. Open mid-Nov–early Apr for skiing (and weekends in May, depending on snowfall). 907-754-2111 or 800-880-3880. www.alyeskaresort.com. Lift tickets begin at $60.

By far the biggest and best-known downhill ski area in Alaska, Alyeska is distinguished by its location near sea level and by prodigious snowfalls, especially late winter and spring. Few are the North American 🎿 ski resorts from which one can admire the ocean while gliding down upper-elevation runs. The area's 1,500 skiable acres offer 2,500 vertical feet of lift-served terrain that ranges from double-black to beginner-intermediate, with a vast array of open bowl skiing up top. Despite Alyeska's proximity to marine waters—which fends off severe cold—the snow is lighter and more skiable than other coastal regions.

Alyeska Resort's Tram

© Hage Photo/Alyeska Resort

The 🚡 **Alyeska Tram**★★ *(runs late May–Sept daily 9:30am–9:30pm; fall and spring hours vary; closed mid-Oct–mid-Nov; $20; 907-754-2275)* rises 2,025ft up a precipitous slope at the resort, taking visitors to a spectacular knob at 2,334ft elevation. At the upper terminal, an observation deck affords wide vistas of Turnagain Arm, the Kenai Peninsula and the Chugach Mountains. A snack shop and gourmet restaurant, Seven Glaciers *(see Restaurants)* provide sustenance and, of course, splendid views. The tram also affords access to alpine hiking trails in summer, when it runs at half-speed to allow better scenic viewing and wildlife watching.

Alaska Wildlife Conservation Center★★

Mile 79, Seward Hwy. (Rte. 1). Open Jan–Feb weekends only; Mar–mid-May daily 10am–6pm; late May–mid-Sept daily 8am–8pm; late Sept–Jan 1 daily 10am–5pm; $10. 907-783-2025. www.alaskawildlife.org. Opened originally as a "game farm" where injured animals could be rehabilitated, this 140-acre facility on the flats at the uppermost end of Turnagain Arm has blossomed into a full-fledged conservation center. Huge natural enclosures hold coastal brown bears, elk, moose, black bears, musk-ox and other indigenous northlands animals. Of special interest is the center's herd of **wood bison**, massive ungulates once native to the Alaska interior; the herd is intended as the source for reintroduction of these land mammals to the wild.

Portage Glacier★

Visitor Center at Mile 1, Portage Glacier Rd. Open mid-May–mid-Sept daily 9am–6pm. $5. 907-783-2326. www.fs.usda.gov/chugach. Once upon a time this well-known natural feature was easily reached by a short drive up an access road off the Whittier Highway; the federal government (it's on Chugach National Forest land) sited the **Begich/Boggs Visitor Center** here in 1986. Then climate change wreaked its effects on the glacier, which has retreated far up its valley, out of sight of the visitor center. Today, visitors must paddle themselves across the terminal lake to view the glacier, or avail themselves of **boat tours** *(depart five times daily mid-May–mid-Sept; $34; 800-544-2206; www.portage glaciercruises.com)*.

Crow Creek Mine

Crow Creek Rd.; follow signs at Girdwood turnoff from Seward Hwy., 38mi south of downtown Anchorage. Open mid-May–mid-Sept daily 9am–6pm. $10 ($20 panning fee). 907-229-3105. www.crowcreekmine.com. This family-owned attraction represents both a historic (1896) gold-mining operation and an ongoing one in which visitors can take part. Rather than 🥇 **pan for gold** in "salted" gravel tubs, here one pans in Crow Creek, so local enthusiasts can and do go home with worthy finds. It's unlikely amateurs will enjoy such luck (successful panning involves considerable skill), but it's an engaging outdoor activity in a beautiful setting.

SOUTH-CENTRAL ALASKA★★

South of the Alaska Range, the land gentles into fertile valleys and rolling forests before abruptly buckling into another cordillera of glacier-capped peaks along the Gulf of Alaska. Land, sea and sky meet in this diverse region where goats clamber on steep cliffs in sight of spouting whales, and fishing villages reap the bounty of spawning salmon.

The ice-free ports of Valdez (*val-DEEZ*), Seward, Homer and Kenai were staging points for exploitation of copper, coal and gold. In the 1910s the railroad linked Seward with Anchorage, but not until the 1950s did a highway traverse the 225mi from Anchorage to Homer. The region continues to recover from the catastrophic *Exxon Valdez* **oil spill** of 1989, which affected more than 1,500mi of shoreline from Prince William Sound to Kodiak Island. Bordered by Cook Inlet, **Turnagain Arm** and Prince William Sound, the **Kenai Peninsula★★**, south of Anchorage, embodies an easily accessible landscape of towering snowy peaks, massive (but shrinking) glaciers, rushing rivers full of salmon, charming seaside towns, sparkling bays, and coves ideal for boating and wildlife watching. Unlike much of the rest of Alaska that offers

Alaska Railroad along Turnagain Arm

©Nicole Geils/Visit Anchorage

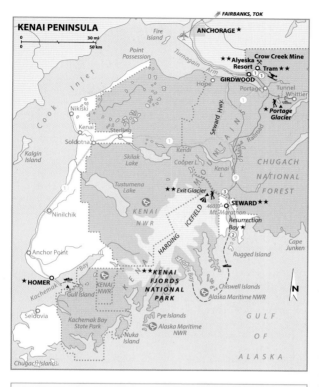

KENAI PENINSULA

FAIRBANKS, TOK
ANCHORAGE ★
Fire Island
Point Possession
Turnagain Arm
★ ★ Alyeska Resort
Crow Creek Mine
○ Tram ★ ★
GIRDWOOD ●
Portage
Tunnel
Whittier
★ Portage Glacier
Cook Inlet
Nikiski ○
Kenai ○
Sterling ○
Soldotna ○
Kalgin Island
Skilak Lake
Kenai
Cooper L.
Kenai L.
CHUGACH NATIONAL FOREST
Tustumena Lake
★ ★ Exit Glacier
HARDING ICEFIELD
4603?
Mt. Marathon
SEWARD ★ ★
Resurrection Bay ★
KENAI NWR
Ninilchik ○
Anchor Point ○
Cape Junken
Rugged Island
★ HOMER ●
Kachemak Bay
Gull Island
KENAI NWR
★ ★ KENAI FJORDS NATIONAL PARK
Chiswell Islands
Alaska Maritime NWR
Seldovia ○
Kachemak Bay State Park
Pye Islands
Alaska Maritime NWR
GULF OF ALASKA
Nuka Island
Chugach Islands
N

HOTELS		RESTAURANT
Alyeska Hotel.......... ①	Seward Windsong Lodge........ ③	Seven Glaciers Restaurant.... ①
Kenai Fjords Wilderness Lodge........ ②		

similar attractions, this famous bulge of land can be reached by road, with Alaska Route 1 bisecting the peninsula on its way south to Seward. Thus, dedicated vehicle travelers with unlimited time on their hands can reach the Kenai from anywhere in North America— from Key West, the southeastern-most point in the US, it's a two-

week, 5,500mi journey. Famous for wilderness trekking, wildlife watching, winter sports and "combat fishing" during the legendary salmon runs in its rivers, the Kenai is synonymous with wild Alaska at its best—and closest. *For visitor information, go online to www.kenaipeninsula.org.*

SOUTH-CENTRAL ALASKA

77

CITIES

SEWARD★★

127mi (about 2.5hrs) south of Anchorage via Alaska Rtes 1 & 9. www.seward.com.

Perched mostly on high ground at the upper end of memorably scenic **Resurrection Bay★**, Seward is a commercial fishing, shipping and tourism center, clasped between snowy peaks on all sides. Starting in 1902 as the **southern terminus** of the Alaska Railroad, Seward became known as the "Gateway to Alaska." Its buildings were largely constructed after a devastating tidal wave during the 9.2-magnitude 1964 earthquake. Today many travelers board Alaska Railroad trains here for the famous 4-hour **Coastal Classic** journey through the wilds of the upper Kenai to Anchorage (*www.alaskarailroad.com*). Cruise boats tie up in Seward at the start or conclusion of certain summer-sailing Alaska itineraries. A dozen or so hotels and lodges house travelers who come to day-cruise to **Kenai Fjords National Park** *(below)*, to visit the **Exit Glacier**, or to fish on a charter boat.

Salmon fishing draws thousands of enthusiasts to the town in July and August, when several species of Pacific salmon, including chinook, coho and sockeye, are running into local rivers. Charter excursions generally run $200-$400 a day, and include all costs such as licensing, gear, and fish packing for shipment home. To find a charter operator consult the Seward Chamber of Commerce, www.seward.com. The visitor center for Kenai Fjords National Park *(see The Great Outdoors below)* is located in Seward *(1212 4th Ave.)*.

Alaska SeaLife Center★★★

301 Railway Ave. Open mid-May–mid-Sept daily 9am–6:30pm (Fri–Sun 8am). Rest of the year daily 10am–5pm. Closed Thanksgiving Day and Dec 25. $22. 907-224-7908. www.alaskasealife.org

Built with funds from the *Exxon Valdez* disaster settlement, the

Giant Pacific octopus, Alaska SeaLife Center

only aquarium in Alaska is a compact facility that enjoys a splendid site along the shores of Resurrection Bay. While it focuses on conservation of Alaska's marine ecosystems—and includes an evenhanded but frank exhibit on the 1989 oil spill—its overall emphasis is on exposing visitors to the rich diversity of the North Pacific marine environment. Touch tanks hold vividly colored sea stars and evanescent nudibranchs; a large enclosure is home to puffins, kittiwakes, ducks and other shorebirds. Below-ground viewing galleries provide an underwater perspective on birds, otters and seals. Behind-the-scenes **tours★★** allow visitors to experience up-close encounters with the charismatic marine mammals who are the stars of the show at the center.

Elsewhere, **ASLC researchers** use remote cameras and tracking devices to study the behavior of wild marine mammals in the Gulf of Alaska; their camera feeds are often on display for visitors to watch.

HOMER★

At the south end of Rte. 1, 222 mi (4 hrs) southwest of Anchorage. www.homeralaska.org.
Celebrated on American public radio by humorist Tom Bodett, Homer is famed as a quirky, artsy and charming town with a unique character. Perched beside Kachemak Bay, literally at the end of the road on the Kenai Peninsula, it features small cafes, art and craft galleries and local oddment shops, most set along **Homer Spit**, a 4.5mi finger of land (actually the remnants of a glacial moraine) stretching into the bay.

Pratt Museum★

3779 Bartlett St. Open mid-May–mid-Sept daily 10am–6pm. Rest of year Tue–Sun noon–5pm. Closed Jan. $10. 907-235-8635. www.prattmuseum.org.
This compact, award-winning museum endeavors to present a well-rounded view of the **Kachemak Bay** region, from its rich indigenous natural history to the stories of the people who have lived here for thousands of years. Wildlife, forest resources and climate are covered in concise displays; fisheries are examined from both the ecological and commercial point of view. A frank overview of the **Exxon Valdez** oil spill disaster is perhaps Alaska's most outspoken exhibit on the 1989 event that devastated the natural environment of the region. Outside, a **botanical garden** and **homestead cabin** illustrate the beauties and challenges of life at the south end of the Kenai Peninsula. A forest trail leads into a nearby rain forest, rare for this part of Alaska.

TALKEETNA

113mi north of Anchorage along Rte. 3, the George Parks Hwy. and Talkeetna Spur Rd. 800-660-2688. www.talkeetnadenali.com.
Variously described as quaint, quirky, charming and appealing, this modest town of 2,600 residents enjoys a lovely site just above the Susitna River. When the weather is regionally fair, the **view of Denali** from the river's shores is spectacular. The Denali National Park Ranger Station here largely serves mountain climbers, but has interpretive exhibits on the mountain and park.

THE GREAT OUTDOORS

Kenai Fjords National Park★★

Visitor center in Seward at 1212 4th Ave. Open Memorial Day–Labor Day daily 8:30am–7pm. Early May and Sept daily 9am–5pm. 907-422-0500. www.nps.gov/kefj.

A stunning landscape of rugged peaks, U-shaped valleys and glaciers forging down from the heights, Kenai Fjords preserves about 670,000 acres of wilderness, half of it ice-covered, along the southeast edge of the Kenai Peninsula. Located here are three among the fast-dwindling tidewater glaciers in Alaska, poised at the upper end of long fjords creased into the Kenai Mountains. Bears, caribou, mountain goats, moose and other wild creatures roam the park; whales, porpoises, otters and ocean denizens ply the waters just offshore, in Resurrection Bay and other inlets. Only one road reaches the park, providing access to **Exit Glacier★★**

from Seward at Mile 3 of the Seward Highway. Exit Glacier Road (*closed mid-Nov–early May*) stretches 8.6mi to a parking lot at a small **interpretive center** (*open year-round daily 9am–8pm*) that explains the park's geology, ecology, and the glacial recession that climate change has brought. Signs along the access road and then the glacier trail mark the years the glacier's toe was at various points; it has receded more than 2mi over the past century. A short hike (*1.4mi*) through cottonwood forest brings visitors to viewpoints just above the glacier. Here one can experience katabatic wind (a meteorological phenomenon caused by downrushing cold air off the Harding Icefield above), and enjoy a broad view across the lower valley now vacated by the glacier. The **Harding Icefield Trail★** is a strenuous (*4.1mi*) uphill day-hike to viewpoints overlooking the vast icefield, whose 300sq mi lie

Exit Glacier

© Fiona Ritter/NPS

Sea otters, Kenai Fjords National Park

atop the peninsula like a blanket, lone peaks (*nunataks*) rising above the ice.

Aside from this one access point, most visitors see the park aboard **tour boats** that depart Seward to cruise through Resurrection Bay and down to Northwestern Fjord, home of one of the park's tidewater glaciers. Some tours loop around the bay; others steam all the way to Northwestern Fjord to view a tidewater glacier. Orcas, humpback whales, sea otters, puffins and Dall's porpoises are invariably seen in the water. Mountain goats clamber the steep cliffs overlooking the bay.

Kenai Fjords Tours is one of the oldest, most experienced and best equipped operators in the area; two of the boats are catamarans that enable high-speed, comfortable cruising. Boat captains take care to protect the environment and wildlife, and

Whittier Tunnel

Bored through 2.5mi of solid rock beneath an arm of the Chugach Range, the Whittier Tunnel connects the small towns on the shores of Prince William Sound to the Anchorage area. Originally built only for railroad use during World War II, the tunnel was upgraded (over environmental protests) to a combined rail/vehicle passage in 2000. Whittier has a cruise-ship terminal, an Alaska ferry terminal, and a large boat harbor at which many Anchorage residents keep boats to use for fishing in Prince William Sound.

Access to the one-way tunnel is controlled, with each direction departing once an hour, and driving through it is a truly unique experience—the rock walls have never been lined, and the railroad tracks are embedded in the road surface. It's the second-longest highway tunnel in North America, and the longest combined rail/vehicle tunnel. Passage through the tunnel, which is 4mi west of Portage, off the Seward Highway, costs $13 for passenger cars.

provide thoughtful, entertaining commentary. Some sailings have National Park Service naturalists aboard. *Tours operate Mar–Oct and include lunch onboard or at a remote lodge; $94-$174; 907-224-8068 or 877-777-4051; www.kenaifjords.com.*

Matanuska Glacier

State recreation site at Mile 101, Glenn Hwy. (Rte. 1). 907-745-5151. www.dnr.alaska.gov/parks. Glacier access (private operator) at Mile 102, Glenn Hwy. $74 guided glacier hike; 907-351-7587 or 800-956-6422; www.micaguides.com.

One of the few places one can fairly easily drive near or walk onto a glacier, Matanuska Glacier straddles the glacier's terminus in the valley of its namesake river, which it feeds. The state park near

Downtown Palmer

©Tom Bol/Mat-Su CVB

it offers campsites and a hiking trail that provides great views of the glacier's terminus, which is on private property and accessible only by utilizing the guide service at the glacier's foot. A zipline enhances the adventure, and ice climbing and raft trips are available for the more adventurous.

Mat-Su Valley

43mi north of Anchorage along Rte. 1, Glenn Highway (1hr drive time). www.alaskavisit.com.

South-central Alaska's "banana belt" faces south into the sun and is far enough inland to escape the summertime cooling effects of Cook Inlet. Thus it is the state's most productive agricultural area, famed for the giant cabbages, beets, lettuces and other vegetables that thrive in the never-dark days of midsummer. The area's unofficial but universal moniker is formed from the names of its two big rivers, the Matanuska and Susitna.

Palmer, which enjoys a pleasant site along the Matanuska River, is home to the famous **Alaska State Fair** *(see Calendar Of Events)*. It was largely settled by "colonists" who came here to farm at the behest of the US government during the Great Depression. A compact downtown **museum**—also the site of the visitor center—depicts this history *(open May–Sept daily 10am–5pm; 907-746-7668; www.palmermuseum.org)*. The adjacent **Agricultural Showcase** displays the region's bounty, best seen in early September.

Wasilla is a newer, largely suburban town now famous as the home of former Alaska governor Sarah Palin; her lakeside house

Glenn Highway Overlook, Mat-Su Valley

is the object of much fascination by camera-clicking tourists. As a suburb of Anchorage, it's also the actual starting point for the famous Iditarod sled dog race (*see Calendar Of Events*). The 🐾 **Iditarod Headquarters** has a small museum devoted to sled-dog racing, the historic trail and the race (*2100 S. Knik-Goosebay Rd.; open mid-May–mid-Sept daily 8am–7pm; rest of the year til 5pm; 907-376-5155; iditarod. com*). Though the arduous 1,000mi race dates to 1973, the original Iditarod Trail was blazed as a mail and gold-rush route in 1910 and ran all the way from Seward to Nome. It was along this route that the legendary dogs Balto and Togo, and others, relayed serum to the diptheria-stricken town of Nome in 1925—the 674 miles covered in a breathtaking five and a half days.

Starting line, Iditarod

THE GREAT OUTDOORS

FAIRBANKS★

The "Golden Heart" of Alaska's interior is a thriving small city (city population 32,000, borough population around 100,000) with a compact downtown, the placid Chena river winding through, and a large, well-established visitor infrastructure. Fairbanks residents are demonstrably fond of their home, despite its obvious challenges—long, cold winters, with prolonged periods of below-zero temperatures, and considerable distance to the rest of the US and Alaska's other two main cities, Anchorage and Juneau. The short but fairly balmy summers feature daily highs in the mid-70s, seemingly unending daylight. Residents make the most of the season by biking, hiking, boating, fishing, 🏌 golfing and numerous other outdoor pursuits.

Legend says the town was first settled when a paddle-wheel steamer ran aground in the Chena River at the current site. **Gold** was discovered in the area in 1902, and the city was incorporated a year later in response to the population boom. Small-scale gold mining continues in the area, with coal mining nearby at Healey. Construction of the **Alaska Highway** brought renewed vigor during World War II, as did the building of the **Trans-Alaska Pipeline** in the mid-1970s. The local economy today relies on tourism (more than 300,000 visitors a year) and government. The **University of Alaska**'s largest campus (about 3,000 students) overlooks the city, and two major military bases nearby, Fort Wainwright and Eielson Air Force Base, make their home here. Several vantage points on the campus, which occupies a ridge north of the main city, might afford a glimpse of Denali's summit when the weather is clear.

Fairbanks has several fine golf courses at which visitors can experience one of the area's annual traditions—**midnight golf**. From mid-June to mid-July—and especially right around the June 21 solstice—one can tee off at about 11pm and play through until 3am or so, accomplishing a full 18-hole round.

The **Chena Bend Golf Course** at Fort Wainwright is a well-maintained military links open to the public (*$42; 907-353-6223; www.ftwainwrightfmwr.com*).

The **North Star Golf Club** is America's northernmost course, an 18-hole adventure that golfers will share with moose and birch-scented breezes (*$35; 907-457-4653; www.northstargolf.com*).

Fast Facts

Land area: 7,361sq mi (Fairbanks North Star Borough)
Population: 100,000 in the borough
Record temperatures: 94°F (1994); −66°F (1961)
Average annual precipitation: 10.3 inches
Average annual snowfall: 69 inches
Daylight: midsummer 22-24 hours; midwinter, 4-5 hours

Practical Information

When to Go

Days lengthen in April; weather warms here in early May. By June, daylight is almost constant, and highs reach the 70s. The cruise-ship land tour buses start arriving then; warm temperatures and crowds persist until late August. September can have fewer visitors, 60°F days and plenty of sunshine. Snow falls by early October, and sub-zero temperatures arrive by November. March and April often bring clear skies and moderating temperatures best for Northern Lights tourism.

Getting There

♦ **By Air** – **Fairbanks International Airport** (FAI) *(907-474-2500; dot. alaska.gov/faiiap).* Alaska Airlines *(800-252-7522; www.alaskaair.com)* has flights between Anchorage, Fairbanks and Seattle daily. Onward service includes jet flights to Prudhoe Bay and Utqiagvik (Barrow). In-state airlines include Ravn *(907-266-8394 or 800-866-8394; www. flyravn.com),* which has service to and from Anchorage. Smaller airlines serve the Interior, as most of the region's communities are not reachable by road.

European travelers reach Fairbanks in summer on weekly scheduled charter flights from Frankfurt, offered by **Condor Airways**, a subsidiary of Thomas Cook Group *(www.condor.com).* In winter **Japan Airlines** offers charters from Tokyo for Northern Lights viewing *(www.jal.com).*

♦ **By Train** – **Alaska Railroad** *(907-265-2494 or 800-544-0552; www.alaskarailroad.com)* links Anchorage, Talkeetna, Denali National Park and Fairbanks. Daily service in summer.

♦ **By Bus** – Bus service between Anchorage, Fairbanks and Whitehorse, Yukon Territory, is available from **Interior Alaska Bus Line** *(907-277-6652 or 800-770-6652; interioralaskabusline.com).*

♦ **By Car** – Fairbanks lies 360mi north of Anchorage on the George Parks Hwy. (Rte. 3); allow 6 hours drive time, more if sightseeing along the way. Major **rental car companies** have facilities at Fairbanks International, though many attractions in the immediate area can be easily seen by utilizing hotel shuttles. Adventurous travelers intent on driving the **Dalton Highway** must rent special vehicles from local agencies—major car rental companies prohibit use of their cars on the Dalton. Contact the Fairbanks CVB for information on local rental agencies.

Visitor Information

The main visitor center is Morris Thompson Center, 101 Dunkel St. downtown. Open in summer daily 8am–9pm, and in winter til 5pm. 907-459-3700. www.explorefairbanks.com.

CREAMER'S FIELD

Fountainhead Antique Auto Museum

LEMETA

MUSEUM OF THE NORTH

University of Alaska Loop

AURORA

College Rd.

Aurora Rd.

Danby

College

Johansen Expwy.

LARGE ANIMAL RESEARCH STA.

CHENA HOT SPRINGS

GEORGESON BOTANICAL GARDEN

COLLEGE

Geist Rd.

Tanana

Hwy.

Noyes Slough

Johansen

Chena

Phillips Field Rd.

Expwy.

Peger Rd.

1st

2nd Ave.

8th Ave.

Gillam St.

Cowles St.

Morris Thompson Cultural and Visitors Center

DOWNTOWN

2nd Ave.

Cushman St.

Chena

FEDERAL BUILDING

GLASS PARK

Riverboat Discovery

Pioneer Park Way

Airport

University Way

Airport Rd.

17th Ave.

Gaffney Rd.

Davis Rd.

Davis

Wilbur St.

Peger Rd.

Lathrop St.

23rd Ave.

SOUTH FAIRBANKS

FORT WAINWRIGHT MILITARY RESERVATION

FAIRBANKS INTL. AIRPORT AND SEAPLANE BASE

Airport Way

Mitchell

Mitchell Expwy.

30th Ave.

30th Ave.

Old Richardson Hwy.

University Ave.

Van Horn Rd.

Van Horn Rd.

Peger Rd.

Cushman St.

Easy St.

FAIRBANKS

0 1 mi

0 2 km

METRO FIELD

Sanduri Ave.

N

HOTELS		RESTAURANTS	
A Taste of Alaska Lodge	①	Gambardella's	①
Chena Hot Springs Resort	②	Lavelle's Bistro	②
Pike's Waterfront Lodge	③	The Pump House	③
River's Edge Resort	④	Silver Gulch Brewery	④

MUSEUMS

Museum of the North★★★

907 Yukon Dr., on UAF campus. Open mid-May–mid-Sept daily 9am–7pm. Rest of the year Mon–Sat 9am–5pm. $12. 907-474-7505. www.uaf.edu/museum.

A sparkling, ivory-colored modern facility on a ridge overlooking the city from the north, this superb museum at the **University of Alaska Fairbanks** houses world-class collections of Alaska art and

Rose Berry Alaska Art Gallery, University of Alaska Museum of the North

© University of Alaska Museum of the North

MUST DO FAIRBANKS

Gallery of Alaska, University of Alaska Museum of the North

© University of Alaska Museum of the North

indigenous art and artifacts. Many exhibits commingle old and new, Native and Western, to illustrate similarities and distinctions among the various forms. The upstairs centerpiece is the 🖼 **Rose Berry Alaska Art Gallery★★★**, a vast hall whose holdings span 2,000 years of creative crafts in Alaska—it is the single best such collection in the state. Priceless treasures here include the **Okvik Madonna**, a prehistoric Eskimo work of carved ivory depicting a mother holding a child; a sweeping view of Denali by iconic Alaska artist Sydney Laurence; and an early 20C parka of wolverine, wolf and squirrel hide. The three are practically side by side, affording an opportunity to contrast three completely different examples of the Great Land's artistic traditions. Elsewhere in the museum, the **Alaska Classics** hall displays more Laurence paintings, as well as other mainstream works devoted to the state. The **Gallery of Alaska★** depicts the state's landscape, ecology and history—including a section devoted to the little-known, tragic **relocation and internment of Aleut Natives** from their home islands during World War II.

Fountainhead Antique Auto Museum★

212 Wedgewood Dr. Open mid-May–mid-Sept Sun–Fri 11am–10pm, Sat til 6pm. Winter Sun only, noon–6pm. $10. 907-450-2100. www.fountainheadmuseum.com.
Housing an exceptional collection of more than 55 antique cars and trucks, this 30,000sq ft museum distinguishes itself by placing its cars in context. Many of the vehicles are firsts in Alaska, and some of them are quite rare, such as an 1899 **Hertel Runabout** and a1903 **Columbia Electric Surrey**. The museum holdings include several vintage (19C) bicycles and even a sparkplug collection. Engaging displays throughout the museum describe the events of the times and the cultural milieu in which the vehicles operated. Mannequins stationed around the museum display clothing fashions of the period, for instance. The walls are lined with vintage photos illustrating the history of motoring in Alaska, a context that makes the museum enjoyable even for visitors who care little about antique cars.

MUSEUMS

HISTORICAL SITES

Morris Thompson Cultural and Visitors Center★★

101 Dunkel St. Open mid-May–late Sept daily 8am–9pm. Rest of the year daily 8am–5pm. 907-456-5774 or 800-327-5774. www.morristhompsoncenter.org.
This airy new facility (2008) along the Chena River serves as the information clearinghouse and interpretive center for Fairbanks and Interior Alaska. It combines the offices and public facilities of the Fairbanks Convention and Visitors Bureau, the area's public lands agencies such as the National Park Service and US Forest Service; Alaska Geographic, a nonprofit

©Josh Spice/Morris Thompson Cultural and Visitors Center

Exhibit: How We Live: The People and the Land

Rainbow of the Night

The Northern Lights— 🔆 *Aurora Borealis*—offer one of Alaska's most-sought off-season visitor experiences. The display of colors in the night sky is caused by the collision of charged particles with earth's atmosphere. It occurs most often in two bands near the Arctic and Antarctic Circles because of the planet's magnetic field. Alaska is one of the key destinations for aurora viewing, and **Fairbanks** is the prime locale in Alaska.

While the aurora can be seen anywhere in the state, any time of year that is not subject to 24-hour daylight, by far the best viewing opportunities (and the best visitor facilities) are found in the Interior and the Arctic from early September to late March. Northern Lights tourism brings thousands of travelers to Fairbanks in winter—famously, Japanese tourists who are fascinated by the phenomenon. Actually seeing it requires a bit of luck—both clear skies and aurora activity must be present, of course, and neither is precisely predictable. Since the displays generally occur after 9pm, sometimes as late as 3am or 4am, one must either be awake or awakened. Most lodgings in Fairbanks offer guests a service in which night-duty staff will wake visitors when displays start. Cold weather clothing (also often on offer from lodgings) is a must, of course; so is patience. The reward is a magnificent natural spectacle that will comprise a lifetime memory; the best displays include banners, curtains and swirls of vivid green, orange, red and yellow that can paint the entire northern sky.

Susan Butcher

Longtime Fairbanks area resident Susan Butcher (1954-2006) was an Alaska icon whose exploits almost defy belief. Raised in Massachusetts and schooled in Colorado as a veterinary technician, she arrived in Alaska in the mid-1970s to find adventure and pursue her love of dogsledding. After early setbacks—in 1984, a pregnant moose killed two dogs in her team during the Iditarod Trail Sled Dog Race—she won the Iditarod four times, the only woman to achieve that distinction. Her first title was in 1985, her last in 1990. More incredibly, in 1979 she became the only woman to reach the summit of Mount McKinley by dogsled.

Butcher was diagnosed with leukemia in 2005 and despite treatment, died the following year. Her husband, Dave Monson, carries on the family's dogsledding business with their two daughters on the outskirts of Fairbanks at Trail Breaker Kennels, a popular stop along the Riverboat Discovery tour. In 2008 the Alaska Legislature designated the first Saturday of every March (traditional start of the Iditarod) as Susan Butcher Day. For more information visit www.susanbutcher.com.

agency devoted to education about the state; the Alaska Native Elders and the Tanana Chiefs Conference, the organization representing the Interior region's largely Athabaskan Native peoples who live in 42 separate communities (*www.tananachiefs. org*). Thus, visitors may come here for advice on hotels and activities in the area; for hiking and camping permits; for education about traditional Native lifestyles and the Interior's rich natural history. Exhibits in the center include a walk-through hall, **How We Live: The People and the Land**★★, in which life-size dioramas depict a traditional Athabaskan summer fish camp, an autumn hunting encampment, and a winter cabin with Northern Lights outside. Elsewhere in the center, visitors may encounter Athabaskan women sewing traditional garments, including famously intricate beadwork.

Outside, a pioneer cabin and garden demonstrate early 20C life in the Interior, and a folk-art installation, the **Antler Arch**, frames the riverside pathway.

Pioneer Park★

2300 Airport Way (at Peger Rd.). Open daily in daylight hours; concessions open late May–early Sept daily noon–8pm. Free park admission. 907-459-108. fnsb.us. Billing itself as Alaska's only historic theme park, this pleasant attraction consists of a large collection of historic buildings and artifacts ranging from pioneer log cabins to a reconstructed frontier boardwalk to an early 20C riverboat, the *Nenana*.

The **Big Stampede** show *($4)* offers a sly musical look at pioneer times; the **Pioneer Air Museum** holds antique aircraft and exhibits on early Alaska aviation *($3)*; and at **40 Below Fairbanks** *($8)*, visitors can step into a chilled chamber to sample the dead-of-winter climate. The **Iron Horse Train** is a narrow-gauge circuit circling the park *($2)*; and next door, **Salmon Bake** is a vast restaurant offering innumerable tour-group members, as well as independent travelers, an all-you-can-eat dinner of Alaska salmon and fixings *($35)*.

Canoe and kayak rentals to float the Chena River, a delightful two-hour excursion, are available at the park from Alaska Outdoor Rentals & Guides *(open May–Sept daily 11am–7pm; $41; 907-457-2453; www.2paddle1.com)*.

Riverboat Discovery★

1975 Discovery Dr. Tours late May–late Sept daily 9am and 2pm. $63. 907-479-6673.
www.riverboatdiscovery.com.
Though the boat used these days for this company's half-day tours (an actual 3hr cruise with several stops en route) is of modern design and construction, it does utilize a stern-mounted paddle wheel for propulsion, as did the hundreds of riverboats that plied the Yukon River and its tributaries during the gold rush days. Choose to sit inside, or outdoors where you can listen to the water churning on the wheels. Passengers are regaled with tales of life in the Interior, both historic and modern. Several stops along the river include a visit to former Iditarod champion Susan Butcher's dog kennels, now run by her husband Dave Monson; a pause to watch a floatplane take off and land; and a lengthy visit to a replica Athabaskan fish camp village.

THE GREAT OUTDOORS

Creamer's Field★★

1300 College Rd. Trails open year-round in daylight hours. Visitor center open mid-May–late Aug daily 9am–5pm, depending on volunteer availability; winter hours Sat noon–4pm. 907-459-7307.
www.creamersfield.org.
Once a large family dairy that sold its products throughout Interior Alaska, this 2,000-acre preserve (it's pronounced "Kramer's") is an important migratory waterfowl stopover, particularly in May and early June, and again late August through September, when visitors will see hundreds of sandhill cranes, geese and other transient birds—as well as year-round resident woodpeckers, ravens, chickadees and more. Trails lead along pastures and through quiet forests; volunteer bird fanciers are often on hand to answer questions such as how resident birds survive harsh winters. The **Boreal Forest Trail** *(1mi)* is especially inviting, wending its way through light-dappled birch woods; the **Farm Road Trail** skirts fields in which sandhill cranes are often seen.

🏛 Big Delta State Historical Park★

Milepost 275, Richardson Hwy. Open May–Sept daily 8am–8pm. 907-451-2695.
www.alaskastateparks.org.

Chena Hot Spring sunset snow coach tour

Oasis of Warmth—and Innovation

One of the unique attractions in Alaska, 🏔 **Chena Hot Springs** is simultaneously a travel resort, a historic hotel, a hot springs spa, a Northern Lights venue—and a famous laboratory for sustainability. Owner/visionary Bernie Karl is transforming what had been a sleepy hot spring lodge into a geothermal marvel at which deep wells tapping earth's heat supply all the resort's energy needs, supplemented by solar power. Vast greenhouses provide tomatoes, salad greens and other produce for the resort's restaurant. Karl is expanding geothermal energy production, and plans to sell power to customers in Fairbanks, 60mi away. The resort's power plants pioneered electric power production using a "moderate temperature" (165°F) geothermal resource.

Guests of the resort (**$$$ all-inclusive**) sleep in comfortable but basic lodge rooms or cabins; day visitors to the springs are welcome (*$15*). During summer's almost constant daylight, hiking, biking, wildlife watching and other pursuits lead to relaxation in the large hot spring pool, where the water ranges from 100–106°F. In winter, snow-cats haul guests up a nearby ridge for aurora viewing. Cross-country skiing, snowshoeing and dogsledding will soon be supplemented with downhill skiing. Even at –30 below zero F, guests soak comfortably in the hot mineral water after dark and glimpse the Northern Lights through the mist. *60mi northeast of Fairbanks at the end of (mile 56) Chena Hot Springs Rd.; 907-451-8104;* *www.chenahotsprings.com.*

Occupying what once was a key juncture on the first road into Alaska's Interior, the Richardson Highway, this pleasant park along the Tanana River (pronounced "Tanuhnaw") features an early 20C roadhouse, an adjacent homestead, picnic facilities and exhibits explaining the site's great importance to travelers heading north from Valdez. Still standing is **Rika's Roadhouse**, a legendary

91

Caribou vs. Reindeer

Though they are biologically members of the same species—akin to dogs and wolves—caribou and reindeer are distinctly different animals. The **caribou** is one of the largest members of the deer family, reaching up to 5ft at the shoulders and 500 pounds or more as mature bulls. Present naturally around the globe in undeveloped areas north of the Arctic Circle, herds are largest in Arctic Alaska and Canada, some numbering close to 500,000. Much smaller numbers are found in subarctic regions of Alaska, the Yukon, British Columbia, other Canadian provinces and occasionally northern-tier US states. These latter are a smaller variant known as **woodland caribou**, as opposed to the Arctic's larger **barren-ground caribou**. Caribou graze on lichen and summer grasses, using their large hooves to paw through snow in winter to find food. Virtually all caribou are migratory, moving from summer to winter feeding grounds.

Caribou

© Jacob W. Frank/NPS (CC-by-2.0)

Reindeer are domestic caribou, having first been domesticated by the peoples of northern Scandinavia perhaps 4,000 years ago. Centuries of breeding have made reindeer smaller, with much shorter legs, and non-migratory.

Both male and female reindeer and caribou have antlers, unlike most other members of the deer family. Bulls conduct ferocious contests during mating season, but shed their antlers by December; intriguingly, pregnant females retain their antlers until spring, using them to fend off bulls when they find good lichen patches during the long, harsh winters of the Arctic.

Reindeer sausage, dark and savory and often compared to elk, is common in Alaska; it's made using meat from domestic reindeer that were brought to the state from Europe in the early 20C. Wild caribou is a key element of the subsistence lifestyle still practiced by many Native peoples— but like moose, caribou meat may not be sold commercially.

Reindeer

©Steve Hillebrand/U.S. Fish and Wildlife Service

MUST DO FAIRBANKS

inn operated for three decades by pioneer Swedish immigrant Rika Wallen. A **small museum** maintained by the Delta Historical Society occupies a sod-roof log cabin, and holds artifacts from pioneer life such as dog sleds, timber-cutting devices and blacksmithing tools.

Robert G. White Large Animal Research Station

2220 Yankovich Rd. Open Jun–Aug Tue–Sat 9:30am–4pm. Guided tours daily 10am, noon and 2pm; $10. 907-474-5724 (message phone only). www.uaf.edu/lars.

Sited in a pleasant vale just a few minutes north of Fairbanks, this outdoor complex has large paddocks holding musk-oxen, caribou and reindeer. Though the animals are here for research purposes, the public is welcome during summer months to stop by and peer through the fences, or embark on the guided tours, during which they are able to see the animals up close and learn about their unique adaptations to life in the Arctic north.

EXCURSIONS

GOLD DREDGE 8★

1803 Old Steese Hwy., Fox (9mi north of Fairbanks). Open mid-May–mid-Sept for daily tours at 10:30am and 1:45pm. $39.95. 907-479-6673 or 866-479-6673. golddredge8.com.

This multi-faceted attraction encompasses a National Historic District north of Fairbanks that includes an old gold mine, the El Dorado; a huge dredge, the namesake No. 8 parked nearby; and a historic mine railroad. Visitors learn to pan for gold, hear the rich history of gold mining in the area (which continues today on a small scale), listen to historic fiddle music, watch sluice boxes in action and travel through a tunnel in which a miner demonstrates hard-rock mining.

While waiting for assayers to weigh any gold they have found,

they are fed cookies and hot chocolate. Since the **Trans-Alaska Pipeline★** runs right by the complex, visitors see and learn about the area's 20C black gold.

ALASKA HIGHWAY★★

See map inside front cover.
Take Rte. 2, the Richardson Highway, southeast out of Fairbanks and continue about 94mi to Delta Junction to begin the Alaska Highway (Rte. 2 in Alaska).
Known for short as the ALCAN Highway, this great road runs from Delta Junction, Alaska, southeast to Dawson Creek in Canada's British Columbia, some 1,300mi (ensuing construction and rerouting have reduced its original number of miles). The route parallels the Tanana River before reaching **Delta Junction**, passes Tok and enters Canada's **Yukon Territory**, where it continues as

Practical Information

When to Go

June and July bring the best weather for travel, with long hours of daylight, but the highway may be crowded then and road repairs are usually undertaken. Snowfall is inevitable in fall, winter and spring and quite possible in May and even August. The period of thaw in spring can make driving conditions difficult, but highway advisories are broadcast promptly.

Driving the Alaska Highway

The Alaska Highway is entirely paved and a major north-south thoroughfare year-round.
US and international drivers must have the **proper documents** such as **passport**, driver's license, vehicle registration, proof of insurance, etc. to enter Canada: for Canada Customs and Border Crossings, call 1-800-461-9999 or access online www.cbsa-asfc.gc.ca. Vehicles should be in good mechanical condition; service stations are situated at regular intervals.
The **speed limit** varies from 80km/h (50mph) to 100km/h (60mph) per posted signs. Headlights should be on at all times. For the latest **road conditions** and construction delays in British Columbia, call 1-800-550-4997 or access www.drivebc.ca. In the Yukon, call 511 or go online to www.511yukon.ca.
For **weather conditions** in British Columbia, call 1-604-664-9010.

♦ **Distances** – Along the Canadian portion of the highway, distances are now marked by **kilometer posts** from Dawson Creek, the official starting point of the highway; on the US side, distances are given in miles. For example, Watson Lake is at KM 1,017 or MI 632.
Historical miles are measurements originally used in the 1940s by lodgings along the route; although inaccurate today, these readings are traditionally employed by businesses as indicators of their location. A most helpful source is **The Milepost** (*1-800-243-0495; www.themilepost.com*), which describes natural and historical sights, restaurants and accommodations mile by mile.

Visitor Information

In addition to *The Milepost (see above)*, visitors can contact **British Columbia Tourism** online (www.hellobc.com) and **Yukon Tourism** (1-800-661-0494; www.travelyukon.com) for information, including maps, transportation and location of visitor centers.
♦ **Time Zones** – Upon entering Canada's Yukon Territory from Alaska, visitors leave Alaska Standard Time and enter the Pacific Standard Time zone.

Autumn, Tetlin National Wildlife Refuge

Route 1 to **Whitehorse**. When it reaches British Columbia, it continues as Route 97 all the way to **Dawson Creek**. En route, drivers are treated to views of the Rocky Mountains, the Liard Valley, and the Coast and the St. Elias mountain ranges.

When the Japanese bombed Pearl Harbor in 1941 and landed in the Aleutian Islands, Americans feared an imminent invasion of mainland Alaska. To link Alaska and the Yukon with the road system farther south, the road was constructed in 1942 by joint agreement between Canada and the US. A land route of more than 1,500mi was pushed through muskeg swamps, over rivers and mountain ranges from Dawson Creek to Alaska in just nine months, a remarkable accomplishment by the US Army Corps of Engineers—and a legend in the annuls of road construction. Upgraded after World War II and opened to civilian traffic, it is of major economic importance as a means of transporting the region's resources and the tourists who travel its length.

Below are some highlights of the Alaska-Yukon portion of the trip.

Tetlin National Wildlife Refuge

KM 1982/MI 1229, south of Tetlin Junction. Open mid-May–mid-Sept 8am–4:30pm. 907-883-5312. www.fws.gov/refuge/tetlin.
South of Tok, you pass the Taylor Highway (Rte. 5), which winds northeast to Dawson City in the Yukon. After Tetlin Junction, in the vicinity of Northway, this immense 682,600-acre preserve spreads out as boreal forest, wetlands, lakes and glacial rivers. The U.S. Fish and Wildlife Service **visitor center** *(about 8mi from the US/Canada border)* has a bookstore and exhibits of wildlife and flora indigenous to the Upper Tana River Valley. An **observation deck** with a scope allows visitors to view the topography and wildlife of the refuge. Parallelling the northern boundary of the preserve, **interpretive panels** at pullouts along the Alaska Highway for about 65mi describe the natural, historical and cultural highlights of the area.

After crossing the US/Canada boder (KM1969/MI 1221), the Alaska Highway is signed as Route 1 and passes through flat muskeg country, and crosses the White and then the Donjek rivers. From the latter (KM 1810/MI 1125), a **view** of the St. Elias Mountains is possible.

Kluane Lake★★

Just before Burwash Landing, the road approaches this vast lake, paralleling it some 40mi and affording lovely **views★★**. Kluane (Kloo-ON-ee) is fed by glaciers, the factor in its gorgeous color. To the south and west rise the **Kluane Ranges,** and to the north and east the **Ruby Range**.

Kluane Museum of History

KM 1700/MI 1093 in Burwash Landing. Open mid-May–mid-Sept daily 9am–6:30pm; nominal fee; 867-841-5561. kluanemuseum.ca. This museum is housed in a six-sided log building. Inside, **dioramas★** of native wildlife line the interior, enabling visitors to compare sizes of moose and elk, for example.

Kluane National Park and Reserve★★

Park open year-round. Use fees apply. Vehicle entrances at Kathleen Lake and Tachäl Dhäl (Sheep Mountain). Visitor center at Tachäl Dhäl (Sheep Mountain) at KM 1707/MI 1061 open late May–early Sept daily 9am–4pm. Visitor center at Haines Junction open late May–early Sept daily 9am–5pm. 867-634-7207. www.pc.gc.ca.

Hiking, camping, rafting, fishing and cross-country skiing are popular activities here *(fees apply)*. From the Alaska Highway, the **Kluane Ranges** (as high as 8,000ft) can be seen. Behind them are the **Icefield Ranges**, which contain peaks exceeding 15,000ft. Best known are **Mount St. Elias** (18,000ft) and **Mount Logan** (19,550ft), second in height only to Mount McKinley *(see Denali)* in Alaska, the highest point on the continent.

At KM 1707/MI 1061, the Alaska Highway passes **Tachäl Dhäl (Sheep Mountain)**, a rocky and barren peak so named for the white Dall sheep sometimes seen on its slopes. The highway crosses the large Slims River Delta at KM 1707-2/MI1061-58.

Haines Junction

KM 1635/MI 1016.
At the junction of the Alaska and Haines (Rte. 3) highways, this

Exhibit, Kluane Museum of History

©Kluane Museum of Natural History

SS Klondike in Whitehorse

community sits at the foot of the Auriol Range. About 12mi south of Haines Junction via Route 3, there is a **view★★** of **Kathleen Lake★★**. Returning to Haines Junction, drivers can continue to Whitehorse (KM 1474/MI 916) on the Alaska Highway.

🛶 Whitehorse★

Overlooking the Yukon River, Whitehorse is the capital of Canada's Yukon Territory. Proud of its part in the Klondike gold rush, the community stages a celebration every February called the Sourdough Rendezvous when people dress in costumes recalling 1898. It is also the height of Northern Lights viewing season. The city owes its existence to the difficulty encountered by the Dawson City-bound **Klondike Stampeders** negotiating Miles Canyon. The **White Pass & Yukon Route Railway★** changed area transportation; its decision to end its line at Whitehorse made the site a bustling center for transferring goods to riverboats or overland stages bound onward to Dawson City. In 1953 the territorial capital was moved here.

While in town, board the **SS Klondike★★** (*6 Robert Service Way;*

open late May–early Sept daily 9:30am–5pm; $6.05; 867-667-4511; www.pc.gc.ca). One of 200 sternwheelers that once plied the Yukon between Whitehorse and Dawson City, this 1937 craft, now restored, is the only steamboat open to the public in the Territory. Visitors can see the engine room, wheelhouse, galley, first-class accommodations and dining room. The **MacBride Museum** (*1st Ave. at Wood St.; mid-May–early Sept daily 9:30am–5pm, call for winter hours; $10; 867-667-2709; www.macbridemuseum.com*) has gold-rush memorabilia, Native artifacts and splendid old **photographs** of the Yukon. A 2hr cruise through **Miles Canyon★** on the Yukon River is a highlight (*6mi south of Whitehorse via Canyon Rd.; late May–early Sept daily 2pm, additional departure mid-Jun–mid-Aug 4pm; $30; 867-668-4716; www.yukonrivercruises.com*).

🛶 Vaudeville Revue
Don't miss Whitehorse's Frantic Follies, with vaudeville acts and lively cancan performances; reservations are essential (*Jun–Aug Tue–Sun 8:30pm; $24; 867-668-2042; www.franticfollies.com*).

THE INTERIOR★

The nickname that has settled on this region of Alaska is the "Golden Heart." The region centers on a low-key small urban area whose fame far belies its size. Here is a city whose name is synonymous worldwide with winter cold—even though its summers, though brief, are surprisingly warm and pleasant. Here are vast rivers that wind their way thousands of miles to the Bering Sea, most feeding into the Yukon, whose 1,980 mile length and broad girth led to its name, which means great river in the Gwich'in language.

Bounded by the Alaska Range and Denali's 20,310ft summit on the south, by the lower but equally forbidding peaks of the **Gates of the Arctic** on the north and by countless leagues of boreal forest in the lowland east and west, the region is often simply called "the Interior." Even though it seems far north to most people, **Fairbanks** *(see above)*, the only major population center in the region, actually sits in the middle of Alaska—a fact which, combined with its gold mining history, is one possible source of the nickname. This is a land of great adventure.

Even in **Denali National Park**, one of America's best-known preserves, just one road penetrates the wilderness, and only a small

Blue Bells, Denali wildflower

Touring Tip

The most compelling portion of **Denali National Park**, the area around Eielson Center and Wonder Lake, lies far from the park entrance along the Denali Park Road—85mi in the case of the lake. Visiting these sights in one day is an arduous journey, up to 12 hours by bus. A much more relaxing and engaging plan is to book a stay at one of the lodges in **Kantishna**, a hamlet at the end of the park road. Each lodge provides its own shuttle to Kantishna, with commentary along the way; when guests reach the hamlet, hiking, biking, fishing, flightseeing, gold panning and wildlife viewing occupy the days. Then one can either ride back on the lodge shuttle, or fly back on **Kantishna Air Taxi**, a longtime flightseeing operator in the park (*service mid-May–mid-Sept daily; $195-$305, depending on route and number of passengers; 907-644-8222; www.katair.com*).

Practical Information

Visiting Denali National Park

When and Where to Go

While most travelers find summer the best time to visit Alaska, Denali's peak is often obscured in June, July and August. March, especially early March, can be a better time to see it. There are no guarantees, but visiting multiple potential viewpoints over the course of several days is a good strategy. In clear weather, excellent vistas may be available at two viewpoints along the Parks Highway in Denali State Park *(see below)*, Mile 135 and Mile 163.

Here's the fact that confounds many visitors: Denali is not visible under any circumstances from the park entrance on the Parks Highway, from the main visitor center or from the lower sections of the Denali Park Road. Not until one is well inside the park at Mile 9 is sighting of the summit possible. It is perhaps most famously visible from **Wonder Lake**, at Mile 85 of the park road. Here, virtually the entire north wall of Denali can be seen, base to summit, and millions of photographs document that fact.

Getting Around

From the visitor center *(see Visitor Information below)*, **private vehicles** may proceed along the park only 15mi, to the first main stopping point, Savage River. Along the way, the first sight of Denali's summit comes into view, around Mile 9—if clouds are not obscuring it. Beyond Savage River, access is restricted to the many park shuttle buses that depart from the visitor center complex, or from pickup points in the roadside hotel community. Numerous iterations of **shuttle bus tours** are available, but almost all utilize modified schoolbuses whose drivers are simultaneously guides and interpreters. Aside from various mountain viewpoints, the drive passes boreal forest, subarctic tundra, intricately braided glacial rivers and numerous subsidiary peaks. But most visitors—and bus drivers—are keeping a sharp eye out for **wildlife**. Bears, moose, caribou and Dall sheep are relatively common; wolves, eagles and lynx are less so. Each sighting brings buses to a halt as visitors snap photos, though park regulations bar visitors from leaving the bus except at designated rest stops. Most tours are operated by the park concessioner, **Aramark/Doyon** *(tours mid-May–mid-Sept daily, multiple departures; $37-$169; 800-622-7275; www.reservedenali.com).*

Trip length can vary from a few hours to an arduous all-day journey to the end of the road and back. Advance **reservations** are strongly recommended, especially for travelers who may be at the park only a couple nights. *Visitors with vertigo should be sure to sit on the right side of the bus westbound, and the left side eastbound, as the road clings to steep mountainsides at some points.*

Practical Information

Visitor Information

The visitor center campus includes the park's main visitor center, a cafe, a bookstore, the Alaska Railroad depot and the park airstrip. Staffed with rangers to answer questions, the **Denali Visitor Center★★** has park maps and activity schedules, and exhibits detailing the geology, natural history and human history of the Mount McKinley massif, the Alaska Range and adjoining alpine tundra and boreal forest. A selection of films covering the park's history and ecology cycles through the center's theater. The adjacent bookstore, operated by Alaska Geographic, has a large selection of books, guides, postcards and souvenirs.

Where to Stay

Most **lodging** near the park entrance is offered by several large hotels associated with tour companies such as Princess and Holland America. The park concessioner has two hotels at the entrance village (*www.denali parkresorts.com*); and a couple small operators offer cabins in the area (*www.mckinleycabins.com*). All the hotels and lodges are roughly comparable and offer comfortable rooms, on-site dining and activity scheduling; any one is a good choice for visitors staying here. Visitors who wish a more distinctive experience should consider a trip to the end of the park road at Kantishna. The oldest and most popular lodge is 🏠 **Kantishna Roadhouse**, a complex of cabins and main lodge in a lovely setting on the shores of Moose Creek. The comfortable log cabins all feature baths and sitting porches; gourmet meals range from salmon to pasta primavera. Lodge guides focus on the surprisingly lush ecology of the subarctic tundra. Like the park road, the lodge is open mid-May to mid-September (*$$$, all-inclusive; 32 units; 907-374-3041 or 800-942-7420; www.kantishnaroadhouse.com*).

Denali shuttle bus

© Tim Rains/NPS (CC-by-2.0)

percentage of visitors ever venture far from that road. The rest of the region, from riverside deciduous woodland to spruce taiga to subarctic tundra, is almost completely a trackless wilderness, the home of bears, moose, wolves, caribou and salmon. Despite those surroundings, Fairbanks is a surprisingly cosmopolitan small city with a major university, fine restaurants, a world-class museum and plenty to occupy a traveler who may not care to set foot beyond the city limits. But one should—this heart beats big and wide.

THE GREAT OUTDOORS

Denali National Park★★★

Roughly 125mi south of Fairbanks on the George Parks Hwy. (Rte. 3). Daily service May–Sept is provided to the park entrance depot by Alaska Railroad (907-265-2494 or 800-544-0552; www.alaska railroad.com). The park is open year-round, but the park road is not plowed or maintained in winter. $10. Main visitor center is located at Mile 1.5 of the park road; open mid-May–mid-Sept daily 8am–6pm. Rest of the year daily til 4pm. 907-683-9532. www.nps.gov/dena.

First set aside in 1917, then expanded vastly in 1980, this famous park holds North America's highest mountain, 20,310ft **Denali**, formerly known as McKinley *(see sidebar p104)*. Unofficial statistics suggest that less than a third of the visitors who come to the Denali region ever see the entire mountain, base to peak—it is frequently shrouded in multiple cloud decks, even when the rest of south-central Alaska is clear *(see When to Go)*. The **invisibility syndrome** is so prevalent that souvenir shops sell T-shirts making fun of the phenomenon; if you are among the lucky 30 percent, you buy a shirt signifying that. Further, local folklore adds that only 13 percent of Denali visitors see the mountain, base to peak, from both sides, north and south.

The national park is also known as a haven for **wildlife** ranging from grizzly bears to Arctic ground squirrels. Beyond that, it is simply a huge wilderness preserve—6 million acres—in which human beings are largely occasional visitors. Visitor facilities are few. There are no classic national park lodges inside Denali, which has only one road within the park, the 92mi Denali Park Road. **Kantishna**, an old mining hamlet at the end of the park road, is the only "town" inside park boundaries; it has a few lodges and an airstrip— but is completely uninhabited in winter. Lying westward across the Nenana River, the park entrance sits at Mile 237 of the George

Autumn, Denali National Park

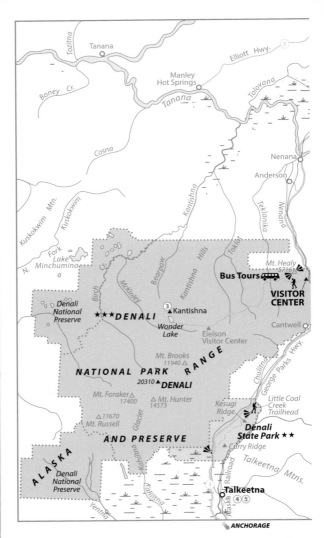

Parks Highway. Yet the summit
of Denali rises far to the southwest,
approximately 80mi as the raven
flies. Around the park entrance
encircles the "town" of Denali,
a congregation of hotels, cafes,

tourist shops and activity outfitters
that bustle with crowds in summer
but are virtually deserted in winter.
Few designated **hiking trails**
exist; visitors are instead advised
to spread out across the tundra,

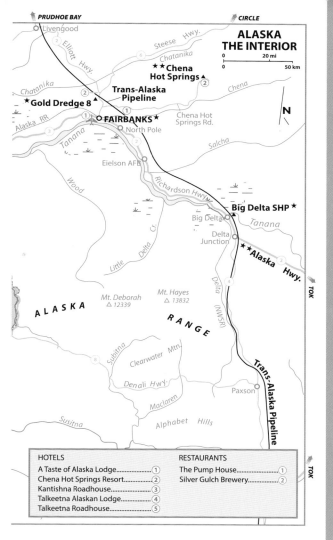

ALASKA
THE INTERIOR

0   20 mi
0   50 km

N

HOTELS

A Taste of Alaska Lodge	①
Chena Hot Springs Resort	②
Kantishna Roadhouse	③
Talkeetna Alaskan Lodge	④
Talkeetna Roadhouse	⑤

RESTAURANTS

The Pump House	①
Silver Gulch Brewery	②

minimizing the impact on any given spot. Permits are required for all overnight hikes.

The two most popular destinations are the **Eielson Visitor Center★★**, at Mile 66; and **Wonder Lake**, a much-photographed natural feature, at Mile 85. A journey to either (or both) is an all-day excursion of at least 10 hours. The Eielson Center, newly reconstructed in 2012, is sited

What's that Mountain's Name?

Long known to Alaska's indigenous Athabaskans as Denali ("The Great One"), North America's highest peak was labeled Mount McKinley in 1897 by William A. Dickey, a prospector who had been exploring the region southeast of Fairbanks in 1896. Dickey decided to attach the name of the then-obscure governor of Ohio, who had just been nominated to run for president by the Republican Party. Both mountain and man later achieved more extensive fame— William McKinley as the 25th president of the US (1897-1901). The mountain was identified by Dickey as the tallest in North America, a fact confirmed by federal surveyors the next year; its pinnacle of 20,310ft is almost 760ft greater than the next-highest, Mount Logan in the Yukon. (And geologists say Denali is growing one millimeter a year.)

So things remained for more than a century—except that, of course, William Dickey did not discover the mountain in any way, and McKinley never visited Alaska, nor paid any attention to a peak named in his honor. Alaska's indigenous people had revered it for centuries, calling it Doleyka, or Truleyka; Russian colonizers called it Bulshaia Gora. The mountain was almost universally still known as "Denali."

Alaskans of all heritages long preferred "Denali." The Alaska Board of Geographic Names officially changed the name to Denali in 1975. Alaska federal legislators often introduced bills in Congress to achieve the name change nationally; many thought it was a done deal in 1980 when the Alaska National Interest Lands Conservation Act significantly expanded the parkland surrounding Denali—but when the dust had settled, only the name of the park was changed to Denali. But the mountain officially remained McKinley until 2015, when President Barack Obama's administration exercised its executive powers and officially changed it to Denali. Now everyone agrees on the mountain's name, and it remains as great as ever. And calling it great certainly fits: its visible base is around 2,000ft, meaning that 18,000ft of mountain can be seen on a clear day—the greatest such mass, base to summit, on earth. Everest, by contrast, tops out at 29,029ft; but its base is at 17,000ft, so its distinct separate mass spans only about 12,000ft.

on a high bluff overlooking the McKinley River Valley and the mountain summit. Built into the hillside, the center is a model of sustainability; compact exhibits explain the park's environment. More notable are several pieces of art, including a huge multi-media fabric "painting" by Ree Nancarrow, *Seasons of Denali*, and a smaller quilt by Linda Beach depicting the East Fork of the Toklat River. Outside, visitors are enthralled by a pair of **interlocking moose antlers** whose erstwhile owners died because they could not separate after a mating-season clash.

For its part, Wonder Lake lies in a low-level basin from which, when the weather is clear, Denali's north-facing Wickersham Wall is visible all the way to the top. Beyond that, at Mile 92, is Kantishna, site of the only lodging actually inside the park (*see p100*).

While it is arguably almost as well-known, Denali is nothing like the Lower 48 parks such as Yellowstone, Yosemite or Great Smoky Mountains. The National Park Service manages it deliberately to maintain its unblemished wilderness character, and the vast majority of visitors experience it aboard a large fleet of buses that ply the park road daily in summer.

Denali State Park★★

Mile 135, George Parks Hwy. (Rte 3). Open daily year-round; no staffed facilities. 907-745-3975. www.alaskastateparks.org.

While it offers hiking, wildlife watching and other outdoor pursuits, this preserve along the Park Highway is best known for two **viewpoints** from which the massive white bulk of Denali can be seen—when the weather is clear. The viewpoints are at Mile 135 and Mile 163, with pull-offs and interpretive board displays at each. Otherwise, this massive park—325,240 acres, half as big as Rhode Island—is devoted to hiking, camping and wilderness exploration. Three public-use cabins sit along Byers Lake in the park, one with an excellent view of Denali's summit.

Dalton Highway and Gates of the Arctic★★

Remote though it may be, Fairbanks is far from the end of the road. That's about 500mi north, past the Arctic Circle along the Dalton Highway, the long wilderness route that was built to serve the Trans-Alaska Pipeline and oil development at Prudhoe Bay. Driving the Dalton is one of North America's last true wilderness road adventures, a 17-hour odyssey that requires both endurance and planning—there are very few facilities along the way.

Major international car rental agencies prohibit use of their vehicles on the Dalton; would-be travelers must rent 4WD vehicles from local agencies. For information contact the Fairbanks CVB, www.explore fairbanks.com.

A kinder, gentler version of the adventure is offered by Fairbanks-based **Northern Alaska Tour Company**; typically, guests fly up to Coldfoot, just north of the Arctic Circle along the Dalton, and drive back, an all-day excursion (*departures twice daily mid-May–late Sept; $359; 907-474-8600; www.northernalaska.com*).

West of the highway, but not reached by any road, stretches **Gates of the Arctic National Park★★**, a stupefyingly rugged range of mountains thrust 7,000ft above the surrounding tundra (*www.nps.gov/gaar*).

The park contains neither roads nor trails, nor facilities of any kind; it is usually "visited" by flightseers departing from Bettles, a small village at its southeast corner (guests must reach Bettles by flying from Fairbanks).

The **Bettles Lodge** offers accommodation at which, in winter, Northern Lights viewing is also often fruitful (*907-479-5111; www.bettleslodge.com*).

REMOTE ALASKA

Called "the bush," vast portions of Alaska are remote from the outside world—not connected to the North American road system, and accessible only by airplane—or, in the case of Valdez in southeast Alaska, by a long, taxing drive from a distant major city. Such disparate compass points include Utqiagvik (Barrow) at the northern tip, Nome near the western extreme, and the south's Alaska Peninsula and Aleutian Islands.

Roadless in Alaska

Of the state's total area of 586,412sq mi, more than half lie outside the main road network—a region, by itself, larger than Texas. Over all, the state has 15,718 miles of public road, and for once Alaska is not only not biggest, it's near the bottom of the list: only five states have fewer miles of road.

This lack of ready access does not mean Bush Alaska is undeveloped, unsophisticated or even uncosmopolitan. It is remote, yes, but not primitive. Wilderness lodges on secluded lakes extend comfort and hospitality to adventurous travelers, as do business hotels in small urbanized locales that afford every modern convenience. Roads do serve many outlying areas: travelers to Nome, for instance, can sightsee for hours on the borough's 350mi of paved roads. Internet service is almost universal: Facebook is being utilized by Native language preservationists to help spread knowledge of indigenous tongues in the Bering Sea. Utqiagvik (Barrow), northernmost community in the US, is a destination sought by adventurous travelers who wish to reach a location rarely visited by mainstream tourists.

Almost every remote place in Alaska, no matter how distant or

Valdez harbor

©Valdez CVB

Practical Information

When to Go

Arctic summer is short. The weather is best in Nome and Utqiagvik (Barrow) mid-Jun to mid-Sept. If you're seeking Northern Lights, March is the best month. Valdez weather starts to settle by May 10, and mid-May through early June is often lovely. Weather throughout the Gulf of Alaska, from Prince William Sound to the Aleutians, begins to deteriorate again around mid-Sept.

Getting There

♦ **By Air** – The main gateway to Remote Alaska is **Ted Stevens Anchorage International Airport** (ANC) (*907-266-2526; www.anchorage airport.com*). *Alaska Airlines (800-252-7522; www.alaskaair.com*) offers most flights to and within Alaska, with almost hourly flights between Anchorage and Seattle, daily service to Portland, and seasonal service to Los Angeles, Denver and Chicago. Onward service includes jet flights to Kodiak, King Salmon, Dillingham, Nome, Utqiagvik (Barrow) and Prudhoe Bay. Other airlines serving Anchorage include United, JetBlue, Delta and American.

In-state airlines include **Ravn** (*907-266-8394 or 800-866-8394; www.flyravn.com*) and **Pen Airways** (*907-771-2640; www.penair.com*), both of which fly between Anchorage and many outlying cities such as Homer, Valdez and Kodiak. All the major remote airports, and many minor ones, have **car rental** outlets that range from local operations to franchisees of international companies like Hertz, Avis and Thrifty; check with the visitors information site for each locale. Taxis are available in most major towns, as many local residents do not have cars. Vehicles are expensive to operate and taxis are not cheap; then again, there's usually not far to go. In Nome, for example, the airport is 1.6mi from downtown, and a taxi ride costs $6.

♦ **By Ferry** – Scheduled ferry service from Bellingham WA to maritime ports in Alaska, including Kodiak, Valdez, Homer and the Aleutians, is provided by the **Alaska Marine Highway System**, *907-465-3941 or 800-642-0066; www.dot.state.ak. us/amhs*.

Visitor Information

Main visitor centers are listed under entries described below.

small, has commercial air service—or a bush pilot willing to fly there. The places described in the following pages all have scheduled air service, either on Alaska Airlines or regional carriers; or can be reached by paved, if lengthy, road. These far-off places possess uncrowded national parks, preserves and wildlife refuges (25 unreachable by road), home to implacable musk-ox, vast caribou herds, immense bears, fish-filled rivers and rugged mountains. They provide unfettered opportunity to hike, paddle, ski, fish and hunt in wilderness that ranges from alpine icefield to trackless taiga or tundra.

CITIES

VALDEZ

305mi east of Anchorage via the Glenn and Richardson Hwys. (Rtes 1 and 4), a 6hr drive; alternate route is through Whittier, then on the Alaska Marine Highway ferry (www.dot.state.ak.us/amhs). Daily flights to and from Anchorage are available via Ravn (flyravn.com). Main visitor center at Fairbanks Dr. and Chenega Ave.; www.valdezalaska.org.

The taxing but scenic route from Anchorage winds its way across two mountain passes through the Talkeetna and Chugach ranges to reach this pleasant small town of 4,000 residents, which occupies a half-mile-wide, 8mi-long bench at the far upper reach of Prince William Sound. A busy port, Valdez became synonymous with human environmental folly after the 1989 *Exxon Valdez* disaster—an unfortunate circumstance for a place that has much to offer. Scenically memorable, the town is set on a sunlit space beneath the 5,000ft peaks of the Chugach Mountains, its harbor's sparkling blue waters providing ready access to Prince William Sound's innumerable wonders.

The buildings are relatively new, as the town was largely destroyed by a tsunami during the 1964 earthquake, and rebuilt on a new site. A quintessentially Alaskan museum, the Whitney, offers indoor interest, and the town's restaurants rely on local fisheries for their menus. In winter, helicopter skiing in the snow-blanketed peaks nearby is popular. In summer, charter operators offer tours into the surrounding marine wilderness. The terminal for the **Trans-Alaska Pipeline** lies across the harbor from the town, but the area has been closed to the public since 2001.

Maxine and Jesse Whitney Museum★★

303 Lowe St., on the campus of Prince William Sound Community College. Open May–Sept daily 9am–7pm; rest of the year by

---

Few People, Lots of Land

A huge expanse of land, remote Alaska is lightly populated. The US Census Bureau estimates that more than 235,000 Alaskans live in "rural" areas, and more than half the state, containing 13 percent of its people, lies outside any designated borough (Alaska's version of a county). Alaska is by far the least densely populated state—1.2 people per square mile, versus Wyoming (#49) at 5.8 people per square mile. Though the notion persists that the state is the last capital of homesteading, only 3,000 people over 90 years ever took advantage of federal homestead laws in Alaska before the program ended in 1986. While there are bush residents who call themselves "homesteaders," today public land is simply sold at auction by the state, or leased for later sale to individuals who stake out a remote parcel and complete a survey and appraisal.

Disaster in Prince William Sound

The hazards of transoceanic petroleum shipping were burned into global consciousness when a supertanker, the *Exxon Valdez*, ran into Bligh Reef on its way out of Valdez on March 24, 1989. The resulting spill of 11 million gallons of crude oil, almost completely uncontained, devastated the marine environment throughout much of south-central Alaska, fouling 1,300mi of coastline in Prince William Sound and as far as Alaska Peninsula. The impact on marine life was catastrophic—2,800 sea otters, 300 seals and 900 bald eagles died; the herring fishery declined; and the state's commercial fishing industry suffered $300 million in damage. A generation later it is still possible to find oil buried under rocks in the spill area. The words "Exxon Valdez" remain synonymous with ecological catastrophe—so much so that the ship itself was sold, renamed several times and finally scrapped in 2012.

Human error caused the accident. To prevent the ship from hitting sea ice, its autopilot was set on a temporary course headed straight at the reef, but was never turned off. Exxon paid a $507 million settlement to Alaska, but many interests believed the company should pay far more ($5 billion); unsuccessful lawsuits continued until 2008. The incident spurred a campaign requiring that, as of 2015, all oil tankers have double hulls. Safety procedures have been upgraded: for example, two tugs now escort loaded oil tankers out of Valdez harbor.

It's a coincidence that the ship involved in this famous catastrophe bore the name of the port from which it sailed. It's also coincidental that the reef it hit is named after the notorious British Navy figure who was the villain in the *Bounty* mutiny—coincidental, but ironic.

appointment. Donation requested. 907-834-1690. www.mjwhitneymuseum.org.
What make this small, nondescript building so charming is Maxine and Jesse Whitney's obvious passion for "Alaskana"—the inspecific term that describes Great Land curios and art. The Fairbanks-area business owners—chiefly Maxine—spent decades accumulating keepsakes, artworks, souvenirs and other oddments from Interior and Arctic Alaska. First they were displayed in a museum in Fairbanks, then moved here to a facility managed by Valdez's community college. The items range from fanciful dolls and ship models to hand-painted reindeer (caribou) hides and exquisite woven willow baskets. Perhaps most valuable is the Whitney's cabinet holding 50 or so hand-carved Eskimo **ivory cribbage boards★**, novelties that enjoyed worldwide currency following the 1909 Alaska-Yukon-Pacific Exhibition in Seattle. Taxidermied animals include a polar bear, musk-ox and moose, thereby affording an opportunity to see up close just how big these animals are.

The museum has no connection to the much more famous Whitney Museum, devoted to American art of a different sort, in New York.

THE GREAT OUTDOORS

Wrangell-St. Elias National Park★★

Straddling the Alaska/Yukon border east of Prince William Sound. No entrance fee. Visitor center sits outside the park boundaries, along Richardson Hwy. (Rte. 4) south of Glenallen at Mile 106; open late May–mid-Sept daily 9am–6pm; winter hours Mon–Fri 9am–4pm. 907-822-7250. www.nps.gov/wrst.

Larger than Switzerland, this massive preserve, measuring 13.2 million acres, is America's largest national park. Yet it is just part of an even larger, cross-border alpine protected area—itself the largest in the world—that is a World Heritage Site, encompassing Wrangell-St. Elias, Glacier Bay National Park, and Canada's Kluane National Park and Tatshenshini-Alsek Provincial Park. Wrangell-St. Elias is entirely wilderness, with

few established trails, and few facilities inside park boundaries save 14 wilderness cabins available for expert trekkers. Massive glaciers, towering mountains, rampant rivers and forests teeming with wildlife are the draws for adventurers.

The centerpiece is 18,008ft **Mount St. Elias**, which is America's second-highest peak. This massif anchors a vast, forbidding empire of ice and snow, the 1,900sq mi Bagley Icefield—largest non-polar icefield on earth when you include its Canadian portion. A gravel road reaches from the Richardson Highway 59mi to **McCarthy**, the small town from which most park exploration launches. Here, the **McCarthy Lodge** and **Kennicott Glacier Lodge** offer fine, historically flavored accommodations, renowned Alaska cuisine and expert information on nearby activities. Just outside McCarthy, the **Kennecott Mines National Historic Landmark★★** is a well-preserved example of the massive mineral extraction that took place here 1911-1938. Nearly $300 million in copper ore was extracted before depletion. The buildings are slowly being stabilized and rehabilitated. Meanwhile, a stroll through the site engenders echoes of a colorful past in a remote locale. From here, the **Root Glacier Trail★** is an easy 2mi hike along the valley edge to the nearest glacier, a 15mi-long, 1mi-wide tongue of ice descending from 13,845ft Regal Mountain. Visitors can scramble up on the glacier (best done with

Kennecott with Root Glacier

©Tom VandenBerg/National Park Service

Mount St. Elias

a guide), or continue another 2mi along the edge, terminating near an abandoned mine facility.

Prince William Sound ★★

Northernmost portion of the Gulf of Alaska; entry points are Whittier and Valdez. www.adfg.alaska.gov; www.fs.usda.gov/chugach.

Roughly 70mi by 30mi, with almost 3,800mi of coastline along a deeply fjorded mainland and innumerable islands, this geographically spectacular marine area is framed by the perpetually snowclad summits of the Chugach Mountains that encircle it. The basin holds more than 150 glaciers, with at least a dozen reaching the sea ("tidewater"), though almost all are receding rapidly. Whales, porpoises, sea otters, sea lions, seals, eagles and millions of seabirds ply its waters; bears and moose prowl its lowlands. Summer salmon runs draw fishing enthusiasts, while tour boats carry camera-toting tourists who gaze in wonder on the landscape and its wild inhabitants.

The sound is reached by exterior road only at Whittier and chiefly, Valdez. Several Alaska Marine Highway routes pass through it on their way to Cordova, Valdez and Whittier. But the best way to experience the sound is on a guided tour boat whose captains know the waters intimately, and whose guides can offer knowledgeable description of the lands, waters and animals within.

Orca pod, Prince William Sound

THE GREAT OUTDOORS

111

CITICS

KODIAK

Roughly 250 air miles south of Anchorage; up to six daily flights to the airport (ADQ) take an hour or less on Alaska Air (www. alaskaair.com) or Ravn (flyravn. com). The airport is subject to fog and other inclement weather: cancelled or delayed flights are common, and it's best not to rely on tight connections in Anchorage, inbound or outbound. The island is also served by Alaska Marine Highway ferries; 907-465-3941 or 800-642-0066; www.dot.state. ak.us/amhs. Main visitor center at 100 Marine Way downtown; open year-round Mon–Fri 8am–5pm (til 7pm in summer if staffing allows); 907-486-4782 or 800-789-4782. www.kodiak.org.

Sitting in the Gulf of Alaska east of the Alaska Peninsula, the "Emerald Isle," as it fashions itself, offers a bracing dichotomy to visitors. Kodiak City, a small portion of the island on the northeast quarter, is a fully developed outpost of human civilization, with an airport, fishing fleet, huge Coast Guard station, hotels, restaurants, theaters, shopping and other accoutrements of modern life—including a local coffee roaster.

A Long Tube of Oil

When the first "oil shock" rattled America in 1973, attention turned to the vast petroleum reserves in Arctic Alaska. If wells could be drilled and turned to production in Prudhoe Bay, the area in which oil had been found in 1968, a huge challenge remained—how to get it anywhere? The answer, the Trans-Alaska Pipeline, at first struck many as a ludicrous idea impossible to engineer. It would have to carry crude oil 800mi to the nearest ice-free port, Valdez, across trackless wilderness in climatic conditions that range from -80 °F to 95°F in summer. It would cross hundreds of miles of permafrost and many more miles of bog, three mountain ranges, 30 major rivers and streams—and before it could ever operate in such circumstances, it would have to be built under them.

An oil industry consortium set about to accomplish just that, and 38 months, $8 billion and millions of man-hours later, the line carried its first oil on June 20, 1977. Since then it has carried almost 17 billion barrels of oil in a pipeline that has 11 pump stations, tops out at 4,739ft elevation, is 4ft in diameter and has walls roughly a half-inch thick. The pipe travels over permafrost on 78,000 supports. Highest throughput was 2.1 million barrels on January 14, 1988.

The line can be seen along the Dalton Highway from Fairbanks to Deadhorse (Prudhoe Bay); and along the Richardson Highway south of Glenallen, most notably around Willow Creek between Miles 91 and 85. At some spots you can stand beneath the pipe and hear the oil flowing through. Interestingly, in more than 35 years, the line has never experienced a spill larger than 16,000 barrels—less than 5 percent the size of the Exxon Valdez disaster, though still damaging.

Surf's up, Dude

Legend has it that an avid surfer was flying to Anchorage one day about 20 years ago, happened to look down an hour before arrival, and noticed big, even waves running onto a long beach 32,000ft below. "Where's that?" he asked someone.

The answer is now well-known to surfers worldwide. **Yakutat**, a tiny hamlet on the shores of the Gulf of Alaska midway between Southeast and Anchorage, has become famous for its reliable but not too massive waves on which wetsuit-clad adventurers can ride beneath the snowy peaks of the St. Elias Mountains. With daily flights from both Anchorage and Seattle on Alaska Airlines (*www. alaskaair.com*), and a modest visitor infrastructure, it draws hundreds of wave-riders, even in winter. The business is sufficient that a local surf shop thrives: Icy Waves (*907-784-3226; www.icywaves.com*) provides equipment, guidance and information for surfers who are looking for an experience different from, say, Waikiki.

With about 12,000 residents, this developed area comprises about 10 percent of what is the second largest US island, at 3,595sq mi. The iconic **Russian Orthodox Holy Resurrection Cathedral** (*410 Mission Rd.*) bears witness to the town's long history: Kodiak was briefly the capital of Russian America from 1792 until Sitka supplanted it in 1808. Today commercial fishing is the major industry; more than 30 million **salmon** are caught around Kodiak Island each year. The town is avidly seeking energy independence and has installed six wind turbines on the ridge overlooking the town. Much of the rest of the island—1.9 million acres—is within **Kodiak National Wildlife Refuge**, a pristine and trackless wilderness that's the stronghold of the Kodiak bear, the largest terrestrial carnivore. The island claims a fascinating ecological distinction: it was virtually treeless until about 200 years ago; now Sitka spruce forest is spreading north to south. A drive down the road

Salmon in stream

CITIES

in that direction takes one from deep forest at one end to open prairie at the other. Though not far from "civilization," it is as wild and untrammeled as anyplace in Alaska, and the refuge is a true jewel among America's wildland preserves. So on Kodiak Island, one can go from wilderness to small city in just minutes—and find both experiences equally worthwhile.

Alutiiq Museum★

215 Mission Rd. Open Jun–Aug Mon, Wed, Thu, Fri 9am–5pm. Rest of the year Tue–Fri 9am–5pm, Sat noon–4pm. $7. 907-486-7004. www.alutiiqmuseum.org.

Though anthropologists consider them closely related to the Inupiat and Yup'ik people farther west, the Alutiiq are a separate indigenous nation that has inhabited Kodiak Island for millennia. This compact museum details their traditional lifestyles, answering questions such as: Where did inhabitants of a treeless island find timber for their homes? (Drift logs) The museum holds a 250,000 item collection of artifacts ranging from etched pebbles to modern Native paintings, though not all items are on display. As with many Native peoples, the museum leading an Alutiiq effort to repatriate artifacts that were stolen or improperly

obtained after European contact. It is itself returning materials to local communities from whence they came.

Baranov Museum★

101 Marine Way. Open summer Mon–Sat 10am–4pm. Rest of the year Tue–Sat 10am–3pm. $5. 907-486-5920. www.baranovmuseum.org.

This modest museum, occupying a 200-year-old house dating from Russian days, offers a broad overview of island history, from the lifestyles of the indigenous Alutiiq people to Russian settlement, statehood and development of Kodiak's fishing industry. Key items include a 19C seal-skin Alutiiq kayak, a bust of Tsar Alexander I from 1804, and seal-skin currency printed by the Russian-American Company in the 1820s.

Kodiak Fisheries Research Center

301 Research Court. Open year-round Mon–Fri 9am–5pm. 907-481-1700. www.afsc.noaa.gov/kodiak.

A major facility of the National Oceanic and Atmospheric Administration (NOAA), this complex is devoted mostly to labs and offices in which scientists are studying, among other things, the effects of climate change on North Pacific marine life. Here you will learn that a phenomenon called ocean acidification may pose as great a threat as atmospheric warming. A touch tank with seastars, crabs and other marine invertebrates, along with a running seawater aquarium holding fish such as salmon and lingcod, introduces visitors to marine species of the region.

Alutiiq Museum and Archaeological Repository
©Alutiiq Museum & Archaeological Repository

THE GREAT OUTDOORS

Kodiak National Wildlife Refuge★★★

Visitor center/headquarters at 402 Center St., in Kodiak. Open late May–early Sept daily 9am–5pm. Rest of the year Tue–Sat 10am–5pm. 907-487-2626. www.fws.gov/refuge/kodiak.

Encompassing nearly 3,000sq mi—about 80 percent of its namesake island south and west of the roaded area around Kodiak—this preserve was established in 1941 to protect the rugged, undeveloped landscape in which 3,000 **Kodiak bears** roam. Generally reckoned the largest of all bears, these animals are thought to have been genetically isolated in the Kodiak Archipelago since the last Ice Age 12,000 years ago. Full-grown males can reach 1,400 pounds, 5-10 percent more than the largest polar bears. They thrive in their habitat because of the relatively mild climate (by Alaska standards), ample range and rich resource base, chiefly the 117 salmon streams in which millions of salmon spawn each year. They are a subspecies of the coastal brown bear, which is itself a distinct race within the brown bear species ursus arctos.

Visiting the refuge is possible only by 🛩 **floatplane** or boat; wilderness guides and outfitters in Kodiak offer various types of services that range from simple drop-off and pickup to escorted pack trips. To find outfitters, contact the **Kodiak Chamber** *(907-486-4782; www.kodiak.org).*

Bear experts Harry and Brigid Dodge operate a remote lodge in the heart of the refuge; situated on a small island in Uyak Bay, **Kodiak Treks' lodge** *(907-487-2122; www.kodiaktreks.com)* uses solar power, avidly practices sustainability, and insists that guests observe bears as unobtrusively as possible. Their philosophy is that the humans are guests of the bears. The lodge accommodates small groups in rustic cabins, and the $350/night rate includes all meals, equipment, excursions and air travel from Kodiak to the lodge.

Viekoda Bay, Kodiak National Wildlife Refuge

© Lisa Hupp/U.S. Fish and Wildlife Service

Bristol Bay Communities★

About 300 air miles southwest of Anchorage. Gateways are King Salmon (AKN) and Dillingham (DLG), with daily scheduled service to each on Alaska Air (www.alaskaair.com) and Pen Air (www.penair.com). Each town has rudimentary visitor facilities, including motels, guest lodges and restaurants; car rentals are available at both airports.

A broad region southwest of Anchorage across Cook Inlet and the crumpled peaks of the Aleutian Range, Bristol Bay is a sparsely settled basin whose lakes and rivers host the world's largest single **salmon fishery**—in good years more than 50 million salmon return here each summer to spawn in the region's freshwaters. The area experiences a tidal wave of people at the end of June as hundreds of commercial fishers arrive to harvest sockeye, coho and pink salmon—and thousands of workers from around the world fly in to man the lines in huge fish processing plants. If you've bought a packaged frozen sockeye filet in your grocery store, it's virtually certain it came from Bristol Bay. However, the ecological health of the region is threatened by a massive gold mine proposed for its headwaters, the controversial Pebble Mine.

Visitors can arrange to observe the fishery—spending a day on a boat, touring a processing plant or both--by contacting the **Bristol Bay Regional Seafood Development Assn.** *(907-770-6339; www.bbrsda.com).*

The region is also home to several top-notch fishing and outdoor recreation lodges. **Bear Trail Lodge** *(907-276-7605 or 888-826-7376; www.fishasl.com)* features a main lodge and five cottages in a delightful site on a bluff above the Naknek River. Cuisine emphasizes, of course, Bristol Bay salmon and other seafood. Lodge guides lead boat or floatplane trips for fishing or wildlife viewing.

A hot tub is poised on a deck overlooking the river; the same company operates a sister lodge on nearby Kvichak River.

Types of Salmon

All five major salmon species—sockeye, pink, coho, chinook and chum—are found commonly in Alaskan waters.

Chum

Sockeye

Pink

Coho

Pink

R. Corbel/Michelin

THE GREAT OUTDOORS

Katmai National Park★★

Northeast end of Alaska Peninsula. Park headquarters are in King Salmon, #1 King Salmon Mall. Visitor center at King Salmon airport terminal; open year-round daily 8am–5pm; 907-246-4250; www.nps.gov/katm. Visitor center in Brooks Camp, 50 air miles southeast of King Salmon, open late May–mid-Sept daily 8am–6pm; all park visitors must check in here when arriving at Brooks Camp. Air travel from King Salmon to Brooks Camp is available from a wide range of operators; the cost generally runs $200 round-trip.

While it holds towering mountains, impressive geological features, resident bears, and rivers and lakes brimming with fish, this vast wilderness landscape is known to laymen as the site, in 1912, of an immense **volcanic eruption**. Novarupta, which scientists estimate released 6cu mi of ash, was earth's largest eruption of the 20C. Nearby valleys were buried 700ft deep. A nearby valley with innumerable steaming fumaroles became famous in 1916 after publication of a photograph in *National Geographic*. Explorers christened the locale the **Valley of Ten Thousand Smokes★**. The fumaroles are largely gone now, but it remains a compelling place to witness earth's geologic forces at work. In summer visitor season, **tour buses** offer an excursion to the valley via the 23mi road from Brooks Camp *(depart daily 8:30am; $96 includes lunch; 800-544-0551; www.katmailand.com).*

Today, the park is equally well known for a different iconic photograph—**brown bears** fishing for salmon atop **Brooks Falls★★**, a 10ft cataract marking the spot that Brooks Lake drains into Naknek Lake. Annual salmon runs here draw large numbers of coastal brown bears to feast on the fish; three viewing platforms allow visitors a safe vantage high above the bears. *Bears may be encountered anywhere in the Brooks Camp complex; best to study park service safety instructions.*

Accommodation at **Brooks Camp** is offered in an attractive log lodge operated by **Katmailand** *(800-544-*

Mt. Cerberus, Baked Mountain and Mt. Griggs, Katmai National Park

THE GREAT OUTDOORS

Bears gathering at Brooks Falls

© NPS

Wood-Tikchik State Park★★

Park is accessible only by air or boat. About 40 air miles north of Dillingham. Dillingham Ranger Station, village of Aleknagik; 907-842-2641; open May–Sept daily 9am–5pm. www.dnr.alaska.gov/parks.

Largest state park in the US, this 1.6 million-acre preserve was created in 1978 not only for recreational purposes, but also to safeguard the portion that is part of the Bristol Bay salmon ecosystem. That land is crucial to the area's Native inhabitants for subsistence fishing, hunting and gathering. The park's two namesake lakes harbor large sockeye salmon populations and other species popular with sport anglers such as lake trout and whitefish. Visitors can paddle, boat, fish and camp.

0551; www.katmailand.com).
Travel packages often include transportation from Anchorage (through King Salmon), meals and activities. Aside from bear viewing, fishing, hiking and canoeing are worthy options.

Please bear with us

Bears are intrinsic to Alaska—over all, there are likely more than 120,000 bears in the Great Land. Alaska has three species:

♦ **Black bear:** This familiar bear, *ursus americanus*, is the same species as those found throughout the Lower 48. Usually black, bears with cinnamon coats are found in Alaska's interior. Mature males can weigh 500 pounds. They thrive on vegetation, fish, insects, small game and sadly, human garbage. It's a myth that they are less dangerous than bigger bears such as grizzlies.

♦ **Brown bear:** Three races or subspecies of this ursine, *ursus arctos*, inhabit Alaska. Largely an interior animal, the familiar **grizzly bear** has a distinctive hump and grizzled fur, and can reach 800 pounds. The **coastal brown bear** lives along the Pacific shores from the ABC islands (Admiralty, Baranov, Chuchagof) to the Bering Sea, and thrives on salmon and vegetation. It can reach 1,000 pounds. The largest land carnivore, the **Kodiak bear** is limited to the Kodiak archipelago; mature males can reach 1,400 pounds and stand 10ft on their hind legs.

♦ **Polar bear:** *Ursus maritimus* is confined to Arctic shores north of the Bering Strait. They can grow to 1,200 pounds, are adept hunters of seals and sea lions, and are under conservation watch by international organizations because of the Arctic's disappearing sea ice.

CITIES

NOME

535 air miles northwest of Anchorage; daily service to Nome airport (OME) is provided by Alaska Airlines (www.alaskaair.com). Visitor center at 301 Front St.; open Jun–Aug daily 8am–7pm; winter Mon–Fri 9am–5pm. 907-443-6555. www.visitnomealaska.com. Car rentals are available at the airport and are highly advised so visitors may explore the region on their own.

Best known today as the finish line for the  **Iditarod Trail Sled Dog Race** each March, this town enjoys a favored site on the southwest side of the Seward Peninsula at the upper end of the Bering Sea. At the end of the 19C, it was one of the many boom towns of the Alaska/Yukon gold rush—discovery of gold here in 1898 soon brought 28,000 people, which made it briefly Alaska's largest city. Tents spread almost 30mi up and down the coast; the timber buildings that followed were largely destroyed in fires and storms from 1905 to 1974. Nome became an important outpost in World War II on the way to Russia;

the current airstrip dates from that time period.

The city's **Carrie M. McLain Memorial Museum** *(223 Front St.; open Jun–Sept daily noon–8pm; rest of the year Tue–Sat noon–6pm; 907-443-6630; www.nomealaska.org)* is chock-full of artifacts, photographs and documents depicting this colorful history. Today, approximately 3,500 people live here; gold mining, tourism and subsistence living drive the economy.

Visitors come to Nome *(largely Jun–Sept)* to witness **gold rush history** such as the 40 dredge remnants in the region; to explore the surrounding landscape, whose tundra is aflame with **wildflowers** *(Jun)* and fall color *(Sept)*. A key draw today is **birdwatching**— more than 150 migratory birds visit the area, and avid birdwatchers especially seek rare strays from Asia not found elsewhere in the US. Nome is also the best place to see musk-oxen, a resident herd of which, transplanted here in the early 20C, roams the region— including the city itself.

Nearing Nome finish line, Iditarod Trail Sled Dog Race

THE GREAT OUTDOORS

Bering Land Bridge National Preserve★★

30 to 50 air miles north of Nome. Visitor center/headquarters at Sitnasuak Building (214 Front St.) in Nome; open year-round Mon–Fri 8am–5pm. 907-443-2522. www.nps.gov/bela.

Aside from the sheer historic value of this remote place—this is the spot where anthropologists believe human beings first arrived in the Western Hemisphere more than 10,000 years ago—it is a striking landscape. Devoid of trees, sculpted by rain and wind, tall grass prairies giving way to low-scrub tundra, it is a memorable locale in which caribou and musk-ox roam, wildflowers carpet the land, and very few traces of human activity present themselves. An amazing variety of wildflowers are found in this barren landscape, colorful varieties such as moss campion, alpine forget-me-nots and alpine azaleas. Plants such as Alaska cotton and even cranberry bushes grow here.

Serpentine Hot Springs area

©National Park Service

The most popular destination in the preserve is **Serpentine Hot Springs★**, a set of geothermal pools out on the tundra, with a bathhouse and small bunkhouse nearby. Because of its biological and geological diversity, the park is a hub for continuing research projects by scientists.

Rolling tundra, Bering Land Bridge National Preserve

©National Park Service

CITIES

UTQIAGVIK (BARROW)

Daily air service to Utqiagvik (Barrow) is provided by Alaska Airlines; www.alaskaair.com. For general information, visit the city's website at www.cityofbarrow.org.

You cannot go any farther north in the US than Utqiagvik (Barrow), Alaska, which rests astride Point Barrow in the Chukchi Sea at 71.3 degrees N. The vast majority of the 4,250 local residents are Inupiat peoples. The **Inupiat Heritage Center** *(5421 North Star St.; 907-852-0422; www.nps.gov/inup)* explains how these hardy people have thrived here for thousands of years, and affords a look at their distinctive arts and crafts. Most travelers who visit Utqiagvik are business people attending to Alaska Native matters; the city is the headquarters of Arctic Slope Regional Corporation, a $2.5 billion Native-owned enterprise.

A few intrepid travelers come for **birdwatching** during the brief summer (there is 24hr daylight from early May to early August), or to dip into the Arctic Ocean, for those who want to say they have

Touring Tip

Visitors flying to Utqiagvik arrive at the **Wiley Post-Will Rogers Memorial Airport**. The town's airport was named in memory of pilot **Wiley Post** and well-known American cowboy-humorist **Will Rogers** (1879-1935), both of whom died in a plane crash in 1935 only 15mi south. Across from the airport a monument to the two men stands in their honor.

swum in every ocean.

In the winter, visitors savor the **Northern Lights**, which may be present 24 hours since the sun sets in late November and does not return for 65 days. Tours of the landscape, including exhibitions of local Eskimo dances and blanket toss, are offered year-round by **Tundra Tours** *(907-852-3900; www.tundratoursinc.com).com)*. The hotel most favored by business travelers is **King Eider Inn** *(907-852-4700; www.kingeider.net)*, where some of the rooms have kitchenettes.

Whale bone rib arc and skin boat frames, Utqiagvik (Barrow)

©Joinna Dewhurst/U.S. Fish and Wildlife Service

CITIES

121

CRUISING ALASKA

The Alaska cruise industry dates its beginning back to 1898, when the Alaska Steamship Company began ferrying leisure travelers from Seattle to Juneau and back, largely for excursion purposes—a novelty in those days. The state has been a key cruise destination ever since.

Each year starting in early May, more than 1 million travelers board ships in Seattle, Vancouver, and several Alaska ports to cruise the shorelines of the North Pacific coast and the Gulf of Alaska—chiefly in the misty, scenic channels and sounds of **Southeast Alaska**. That total represents a population greater than that of San Francisco or Vancouver. More than three dozen ships, representing a dozen-plus lines, make in excess of 500 sailings each summer to the Great Land. One quarter of cruise passengers add a land-based journey to their sea voyages.

A TOP DESTINATION

Cruising is big business in Alaska, and in the cruise world, Alaska is big business. For some companies, such as Holland America and Princess, the state has long been the major foundation of their

business, and continues to be so. As measured by cruise booking organizations, Alaska is one of the top five cruise destinations on earth—ranking third, after the Caribbean and Mediterranean, in one 2011 survey. It is a distinctly different cruise market from most others: Alaska cruise travelers almost universally board their boats to see the sights along the way, as opposed to enjoy warm weather and onboard relaxation. They gather on 🚢 **deck** to watch immense glaciers they hope will calve (shed ice); they marvel at humpback whales breaching, bears prowling the shoreline, waterfalls plunging hundreds of feet into emerald fjords, eagles staring implacably from waterfront nests. Some cruise lines, usually those with smaller ships, have naturalists onboard who give informative talks and answer questions.

Cruise Ship at Hubbard Glacier, Yakutat Bay

©Leslie Forsberg/Michelin

Hoofing it Ashore

Virtually all cruise ships, large or small, make **port calls** at various spots in Alaska—and there is plenty to do in each place for those who don't wish to pay for guided shore excursions. All cruise boats either dock at landside wharves, or if they must anchor in the harbor, provide passage to shore aboard small boats (lighters). In some locales, such as Sitka, the cruise-ship wharf is quite a distance from town; usually the cruise company and/or the local visitor bureau will provide **free shuttles** into town.

All the major Alaska ports of call have worthy offerings for the independent traveler **on foot** (see Ports of Call below). Strolling through Sitka, Ketchikan or Juneau also affords the opportunity to patronize local stores and cafes; get some exercise; and stumble upon unexpected delights, such as a local coffee roaster or a small artists' cooperative gallery. Shore excursions and self-guided port adventures are both worthy ways to experience Alaska's seaside communities—and that's what an Alaska cruise is about.

UNCROWDED SEAS

Luckily, for all the heft of these statistics, there is plenty of room to explore the waters of Alaska. Even on the very biggest ships, travelers will usually spy another cruise boat only in port—Juneau, Ketchikan, Sitka, for example—and in the most popular remote destinations, such as Glacier Bay and Yakutat Bay. The **sheer scale** of the landscape tends to "shrink" even the largest vessels; framed against the Hubbard Glacier, a 2,500-passenger cruise ship seems modest in size. And compared to the vast majesty of Alaska, it is. That's what makes the Alaska cruise experience unique.

Even for seasoned world travelers, aboard any type of ship, large or small, an Alaska cruise is certain to create a **lifetime memory**.

For more information on cruising in Alaska in general, visit the industry's nonprofit organization, **Alaska Cruise Association**, at cliaalaska.org.

COST JUGGLING

Economy travelers can drive down the cost of a cruise with several reliable strategies:

♦ **Interior cabins** are generally much less expensive, sometimes almost half as much as balcony staterooms. One doesn't take an Alaska cruise to spend much time in the cabin; but this choice is not for the claustrophobic.

♦ **Early and late season sailings** are often discounted somewhat. Alaska sailings on big ships start in early May and continue through September; peak season is June 15 through August 15.

♦ **Positioning cruises**, especially on large boats, are often discounted. For example, all the big-ship companies move their ships to the Caribbean or Hawaii markets at the end of September; a sailing from Juneau to Los Angeles may be a bargain (though it will likely include few, if any, port calls).

Choosing Your Cruise

* *Decide first what type of cruise appeals to you most.*

Large Ships - Most common is a **big-ship experience** in which you enjoy huge dining variety, onboard activities such as spas, theaters and pools, along with a wide array of shore excursions in port. This approach has many advantages, but you will be sharing almost all your Alaska experiences with thousands of fellow passengers. Holland America, Princess, Disney, Royal Caribbean, Carnival, Celebrity and Norwegian offer this type of Alaska cruise. Such cruises run from $1,500-$5,000, depending on length of voyage, cabin choice, season, shore excursions and other inclusions.

Midsize Ships - (under 1,000 passengers) These ships tend to be more luxurious, with larger staterooms, but with limitations onboard—there may be only five dining options, for example, and just one pool. The sense of crowding is diminished. Shore excursions remain numerous. Examples include Crystal, Oceania, Sllversea and Regent Seven Seas. Expect to spend $3,000 or more.

Small-ship Cruises - (fewer than 200 passengers) Small ships focus on exploring remote areas big boats cannot reach, but they usually have just one dining room, no pool and perhaps not even a spa. Wildlife watching, environmental education and cultural exploration are the basis of daily activities; port calls may be limited, and shore excursions emphasize outdoor recreation such as kayaking, hiking and fishing. The three major operators are Lindblad Expeditions, Un-Cruise and Alaskan Dream Cruises. Figure on costs in the $2,500 range and up.

Boutique Cruise Boats - With just four or five guest cabins and a total capacity below 20 passengers, these cruises offer a unique, personalized experience in which the captain is the itinerary planner, and the boat goes where the guests wish, to pursue activities as desired, adapt to changing weather or other conditions such as wildlife movements. Examples include Alaska Sea Adventures. Costs vary widely, from $2,500 to more than $6,000 or, in the case of exclusive charters, well above $20,000.

* *Then choose the itinerary you wish.*

Compare it to those offered by the type of ship you prefer. Trip length is usually one week; some passengers stay onboard longer cruises and return south along slightly different routes, thus expanding their experience— Seattle to Anchorage, say, and back, with stops in Ketchikan and Glacier Bay on the way north, and in Kodiak, Yakutat Bay and Sitka southbound. Most big-ship trips depart Seattle or Vancouver and include the **Inside Passage★★** through British Columbia, port calls in Ketchikan, Sitka and Juneau; and visits to either Glacier Bay, Tracy Arm or Yakutat Bay for glacier viewing. Smaller ships generally depart Juneau and sail around Southeast Alaska for five days to a week, including glacier viewing, fjord visits, wildlife watching and a few port calls on their itinerary. Boutique cruises depart from various ports in Southeast, such as Petersburg, Sitka and Juneau.

♦ *Then compare your ship-type and itinerary choices with your budget.*

Global warming has brought dramatic change to the Arctic; one of the most notable transformations is the disappearance of sea ice in the ocean along the Alaskan and Canadian northern coastlines. In late summer, that has opened the route to shipping, and the cruise industry has taken note. Crystal Cruises inaugurated a Northwest Passage cruise in 2016, departing Anchorage and arriving in New York a month later. The vessel was specially equipped for sea ice encounters, was escorted by an icebreaker—and successfully transited a route that had been sought for centuries by explorers. More such voyages are planned by other cruise companies, offering one of the last great adventures on earth.

🚢 Shore Excursions

Long a mainstay of the cruise experience, shore excursions in Alaska offer a diverse array of activities, locales, durations and philosophical emphasis. You can pile on a bus and visit glaciers such as the Mendenhall Glacier, learning about these remarkable geological features and how climate change is erasing them. You can visit a Native carver, watch her fashion raw cedar into marvelous totems and learn about the significance of these famous works of art. Or you can follow a guide on a shopping stroll through portside boutiques. Active excursions are available in virtually all ports of call: kayaking, hiking, fishing, biking.

Shore excursions are costly, ranging from $50 up to $500 or more for deluxe, private adventures such as 🚁 **helicopter flightseeing** and glacier landings. It's worth it to research a cruise's excursion menu before sailing, and make thoughtful selections based on your interests.

♦ **Shore excursions are an essential part of the Alaska experience.**

Some cruise itineraries around the world are designed for guests to have a virtually complete experience without ever leaving the boat—sailings from Miami to the Bahamas, for instance, aboard mega-ships, carrying 5,000 passengers, that are essentially huge resorts that float. In Alaska, shore excursions offer many of the best reasons to take the cruise to begin with—experiencing Native culture, kayaking, hiking or fishing in the Alaska outdoors; wildlife watching in a way not possible on the big boats. Though shore excursions do cost extra (except on some small-ship cruises), an Alaska cruise without them omits a large part of the experience.

♦ **Not all shore excursions are created equal.**

Most ports of call in Alaska have numerous tour companies whose buses stand ready to scoop up cruise passengers each morning and take them to this or that museum, Native carving center, salmon-bake restaurant or shopping district. Travel rating websites, and in particular cruise-rating websites such as cruisecritic.com, maintain extensive catalogs of reviews of shore excursions, comment boards and so forth—a few hours spent consulting them is worth it.

- **Cruise industry sales** in general occur during certain times of year—the period after Christmas through January is a good time to shop, so much so that it has acquired the moniker "wave season."

- **Packages** don't necessarily drive down the actual cruise cost, but can save money overall if you book a sailing along with airfare and a land excursion (to Denali National Park, say) through the cruise company. Cruise sales representatives are very eager to do this; but it's not a bargain if you would otherwise not take a Denali side trip, or hop a bus up to the Yukon.

- **"Unbundling"** has swept the cruise industry, and it's easy to **save money onboard** by avoiding optional spending. Commemorative photographs, bottles of champagne, sessions at the blackjack table, elaborate shore excursions—all add significantly to the actual cost of a cruise. No, shopping onboard is not a bargain; neither is shopping onshore at most ports of call. Premium dining aboard most ships is pleasant—and cruise companies have vastly improved the quality of their fine dining—but it's not the same as premium dining back home. If you're on a budget, keep the $30 premium in your wallet. Alaska cruise fares still include all the basics: a berth, access to most onboard facilities, unlimited cafeteria dining, and the ability to simply walk ashore in port. Circumspect travelers can save 30 percent or more.

🛳 PORTS OF CALL

Most major Alaska cruise ports of call are detailed elsewhere in this guide, with best attractions in each, plus hotels and restaurants for those overnighting in such cities as Juneau, Seward or Anchorage. First-time Alaska cruisers endeavoring to choose among potential itineraries are advised to read the relevant sections; consult rating websites such as cruisecritic.com, and select according to their tastes and interests. Here's a rundown of the major ports of call and their key characteristics, plus best shore excursions and the best sights that can be reached on foot for those who bypass shore excursions:

Ketchikan

Jumping-off point for Misty Fiords National Monument, excellent city museum, two splendid Native culture centers on the outskirts. Best shore excursions: Saxman Native Village,

Cruises and Alaska's Economy

The cruising industry composes a significant portion of the Alaska economy, and an even greater portion of Alaska's tourism industry—more than half by number of visitors, more than 60 percent by dollar volume in the roughly $1.8 billion tourism industry. Cruise passenger spending contributes almost $600 million to the state economy (not counting the cost of the cruise itself).

Aboard *Northern Song*

"OK, here's what real Alaska shrimp fanciers do." Dennis Rogers, captain of the *MV Northern Song* and owner of Alaska Sea Adventures (ASA), is standing on the back deck of his boat, demonstrating to his passengers how to make instant prawn sushi from a batch of Alaska spot prawns just caught: "strip off the shell, wolf down the shrimp, savor." The salt smell sharpens the air. On the deck is the shrimp pot he's used, baited with herring, to catch the prawns. Mist curls around this back channel of Sitka Sound. A humpback whale surfaces a mile away, and Rogers hurries up to the wheelhouse to set course for the chance at close-up whale photography.

The moment exemplifies ultra-small-ship cruising in Southeast Alaska. Life aboard a boutique cruise (sometimes called a private cruise) such as that offered by ASA, is a much different experience from the massive, multi-thousand-passenger ships that sail Alaska throughout the summer. The staterooms, though smaller than those aboard big boats, are cozy and well outfitted—yet you'll be in your berth only to sleep. Dinner brings all onboard to a spiffy dining room/lounge/galley in which the chef is literally a few feet away as you watch him work; supper may include seafood caught that day by the crew (or guests).

The itinerary and activities are infinitely more flexible than on large ships. If passengers want to duck into a tiny channel to photograph a gathering of bald eagles watching herring spawn, that's where Rogers will go (if it's navigable). If the wind is kicking up large swells in open sounds, off he'll head into a back bay for an afternoon hiking a sandy beach. If passengers want to stop off in Wrangell for pizza, that's possible too.

The *Northern Song*, a refitted yacht, is highly seaworthy, comfortable and stable. Itineraries run from March through a unique late autumn whale-watching trip. Costs range from $3,00 per person up to $6,000. For more information on Northern Song, visit *www.yachtalaska.com*. For other boutique cruises, visit *www.travelalaska.com*.

Potlatch Totem Park. On foot: Southeast Alaska Discovery Center, Totem Heritage Center.

Sitka

Alaska center for Russian-American history; most important sights are within walking distance for cruise passengers. Best excursions: Alaska Raptor Center, Sitka Sound boat tours. On foot: Sitka National Historical Park, Sheldon Jackson Museum, St. Michael's Cathedral, New Archangel Dancers.

Juneau

Alaska capital city, impressive gold-mining history. Best excursions: Mendenhall Glacier, either by bus or flightseeing; Last Chance Mining Museum; Macaulay fish hatchery; harbor tours. On foot: Alaska State Museum, Mount Roberts Tram, Juneau-Douglas City Museum.

Skagway

Gold rush history center, well-preserved historic city center, jumping-off point for Yukon land

Alaska by Sea Bus

Given the few roads in Southeast Alaska, transportation by plane and boat is the norm. Voyaging by water can be a memorable part of an Alaskan vacation in itself—witness the success of the cruise industry.

The ferries of the **Alaska Marine Highway System** *(907-465-3941 or 800-642-0066; www.dot.state.ak.us/amhs)* are used by commuters and sightseers alike. The ferry system links 17 towns in the Panhandle, south-central Alaska and the Aleutian islands with Bellingham, Washington, with major stops along the **Inside Passage**—the 1,000mi waterway from Seattle to Skagway. These ferries typically make for a less expensive travel option than luxury cruises (or commercial airlines). Naturalists are often onboard in the summer to interpret marine mammal and bird life. Comfortable overnight cabins are available; if you plan to book a cabin, or transport a car in summer, it's advisable to reserve many months ahead. Port stops generally are brief. Some passengers bring a kayak or bicycle aboard, adding an adventure option for a small fee.

tours. Best shore excursions: White Pass and Yukon Route Railroad. On foot: Klondike Gold Rush National Historical Park.

Kodiak
Commercial fishing center, gateway to Kodiak National Wildlife Refuge. Best shore excursions: Kodiak bear watching. On foot: Alutiiq Museum.

Seward
Commercial fishing and glacier touring center, gateway to Kenai Fjords National Park and on Alaska Railroad, to Anchorage and Interior. Best shore excursions: Resurrection Bay boat tours; Exit Glacier tours. On foot: Alaska SeaLife Center.

Haines
Distinctive small city with beautiful setting and sunny summer weather. Best excursions: Klukwan Jilkaat Kwaan Heritage Center; Chilkat river rafting; Kroschel Wildlife Center. On foot: American Bald Eagle Foundation.

Kodiak in summer

© U.S. Fish and Wildlife Service

© Michael S. Nolan/agefotostock

Humpback whales

A WHALE OF A SIGHT

Of all the sights to be seen in Alaska, the most sought is likely the spectacle of a great **whale breaching**—leaping out of a blue sea in Southeast Alaska, snow-capped peaks in the background, the calm water mirroring the scene. Fortunately, thousands of visitors get their wish each summer in **Southeast Alaska**, whose inlets, bays and channels may be the best whale-watching territory in the world.

Each spring, hundreds of 30- to 60-ft **humpback whales** arrive from Hawaii to feed and rear their young in the food-rich waters of the Gulf of Alaska. The whales show up in late March, as billions of herring start to spawn; most whales remain until September or October. **Gray whales** also head north to Alaska in the spring from Mexico, also enjoying the wealth of food on which to raise their young. Sometimes seen in inside waters, they more often remain "outside" in nearshore ocean bays and channels. And both resident and transient **orca whale** populations

cruise these waters, feeding on the abundant salmon and marine mammal stocks.

Dozens of **tour boats** depart each day from the harbors in Juneau, Ketchikan, Sitka and several smaller ports in the Southeast. Despite the large numbers of boats and visitors, the experience here is very different from other famous whale-watching areas such as Puget Sound. The vast territory spreads the impact; and the region's tour operators observe **stringent protocols** to protect marine life.

Tour boats do not approach closer than 100 yards to marine mammals; do not chase, encircle or otherwise hinder the whales; don't "stay on" a particular group of whales for lengthy periods; and avoid gathering in groups around whales. Most boats are larger catamarans with inboard engines that vastly reduce the **underwater noise** the whales experience (as opposed to the horrific noise created by open rafts with high-speed outboard engines).

129

Brown bear cub

© Hillebrand, Steve/U.S. Fish and Wildlife Service

The Brown Bears of Pack Creek

For centuries the 1,600 coastal brown bears on **Admiralty Island**, southeast of Juneau, have been feasting on clams, sedges and salmon in and along **Pack Creek**, a small drainage at the north end of the island. For 80 years, humans have been coming here to watch the bears, and the delicate balance between the two is a bear-viewing venue unique in North America. Here, humans are the guests. Required to obtain permits, they are confined to a small viewing area and restricted in number (no more than 12 per group) as well as behavior (viewers may bring no food of any kind, for example, and must stay in their group). The bears are the residents, going about their daily lives as they always have.

Visitors are escorted by state or federal guides, a practice that fosters unusual experiences that, elsewhere, would be cause for alarm. Here, for example, proximity to mother bears with cubs is common and not a reason to retreat. Bears sometimes approach quite close to the viewing area. But, for generations, the bears have become habituated to this unique arrangement; to date, there has never been a single conflict. For more information visit *recreation.gov*.

It's best to utilize Juneau-based tour operators who take visitors to the viewing area, accompanied by naturalist guides. **Above & Beyond Alaska** *(beyondak.com)* provides transportation, permits, guides and interpretation and offers the unparalleled experience of kayaking or canoeing in the Pack Creek inlet. Other tour operators can be found via the Juneau tourism office *(www.traveljuneau.com)*.

Virtually all whale-watching tours spy whales. Lucky visitors may see humpbacks **bubble netting**— using expelled breath to encircle schooling food fish in a "net" of bubbles and drive them to the surface. It's an amazing sight, but so is any glimpse of a great whale in Southeast Alaska waters. One of the biggest and best operators is **Allen Marine Tours**, a family-owned company that sails comfortable catamarans daily from Juneau, Sitka and Ketchikan using knowledgeable local guides and captains *(www.allenmarinetours. com)*. Other tour operators can be found through local tourist offices, or by consulting your cruise ship's excursion desk.

FOR KIDS

The vast open spaces of Alaska can be great teaching tools for children. Spotting a bald eagle or a moose in the distance or a colorful wildflower no doubt makes for a memorable experience. As for urban diversions, here are some attractions kids of all ages will enjoy. Find them in the city shown in bold.

Alaska SeaLife Center★★★
Seward boasts the only aquarium in the state. Along with the usual marine life, you'll find otters, seals, and Steller sea lions.

Alaska Raptor Center★★
Kids meet eagles at this Sitka standout. Nearby, the **Sitka Sound Science Center** has touch tanks with anemones, seastars and more.

Alaska Zoo★
Anchorage's zoo has Alaska's wild animals like musk-oxen, Dall sheep and wolves, as well as tigers, snow leopards and wolverines from other parts of the world.

Last Chance Mining Museum
Youngsters can pan for gold in the creek near historic mine buildings just north of **Juneau**.

Pioneer Park★
In **Fairbanks** kids can enter a chilled chamber called 40 Below Fairbanks to get a feel for Alaska's cold winter temperatures.

Riverboat Discovery★
Kids will jump at the chance to ride the top deck of a paddle-wheeler along **Fairbanks**' Chena River.

Saxman Native Village★
In **Ketchikan** children can step inside a bighouse, watch carvers work with wood and see traditional Native dances.

White Pass & Yukon Route Railroad★★
Kids will hold on to their seats when **Skagway**'s famous train rounds sharp curves and chugs up steep grades.

Playful Steller sea lions, Alaska SeaLife Center

© Alaska SeaLife Center

RESTAURANTS

Given the huge travel industry and the need for wintertime respite from the cold and dark, tourism officials estimate that there are more restaurants per capita in Alaska than in the other 49 US states. Where there's demand, supply widens. Alaska gourmet chefs have been fashioning a regional cuisine in the past decade, and the best restaurants focus on local food as much as practical, like blueberry-glazed, pan-roasted sockeye salmon, say. Travelers wishing to experience the Great Land in every possible aspect should endeavor to dine on authentic Alaskan foods—and ask to be sure.

PRICES AND AMENITIES

The restaurants listed below were selected for their ambience, location and/or value for money. Rates indicate the average cost of an appetizer, an entrée and a dessert for one person (not including tax, gratuity or beverages). Most restaurants are open daily (except where noted) and accept major credit cards. Call for information regarding reservations, dress code and opening hours.

Luxury	$$$$	over $75
Expensive	$$$	$50 to $75
Moderate	$$	$25 to $50
Inexpensive	$	less than $25

CUISINE

The foundation of Alaska cuisine is, of course, **seafood**—salmon, halibut, cod, crab, shrimp and other catch. There are five kinds of Pacific **salmon**, each known by two names: king (chinook) and sockeye (red) are generally considered best for eating; followed by silver (coho), pink (humpy) and chum (dog salmon). Preparations usually consist of roasting the fish with oil or butter, or cooking it over a wood fire of alder, cottonwood or other hardwood, the traditional Native preparation.

In Alaska three types of **crab** are common—snow, king (Tanner) and Dungeness. While the first two are best-known and most-sought outside Alaska, many residents prefer the taste of Dungeness, partly because virtually all king and snow crab is frozen onboard the boat right after being caught. Thus, almost none served in restaurants is fresh.

Lingcod, halibut, rockfish, true cod and many other saltwater species are often on menus; so are Alaska-raised oysters, clams and scallops. Alaska **spot prawns** (shrimp) are a great delicacy; alas, most shrimp served in the state is farm-raised in Asia, as in the rest of the US. Alaska shrimp will be identified as such. The state's **agricultural industry** is small but vigorous—local producers north of Anchorage and in the Tanana Valley outside Fairbanks grow cool weather crops such as kale, beets, potatoes and salad greens, plus greenhouse tomatoes and squash. Alaska is famous for giant cabbages that surpass 100 pounds in the long days of midsummer. Resident farmers sell under the brand "**Alaska Grown**"—look for the distinctive blue, green and yellow emblem at restaurant entrances. Foragers pick vast quantities of wild blueberries in late summer, some of which are sold to commercial cooks.

Reindeer (domesticated caribou) is produced by farmers in several areas of the state, and the meat often appears on menus. It is darker and more savory than venison, often likened to elk; reindeer sausage is ubiquitous and commonly found at street vendor food carts.

A new wrinkle in Alaska is a collection of distilleries in Fairbanks, Anchorage and Haines that prepare spirits such as vodka flavored with spruce tips, sometimes using Alaska-grown barley. In particular, Juneau's **Alaskan Brewing** (*www.alaskanbeer.com*) produces Alaskan Amber and other craft beers that are found throughout the state and the Western US. Anchorage has a half-dozen brewpubs, but their products are sold mostly on-site.

Aside from these items, virtually all food and drink in Alaska is shipped in from elsewhere—meat, produce, milk, staples such as flour, oil and butter. Thus, if you have a steak in Juneau or fried chicken in Anchorage, the meat almost certainly came from as far away as Iowa or Arkansas. Ice cream may be handmade, but the milk is from California. Even items one may think are Alaskan may not be—the berries in blueberry pancakes, for example, are often from California.

RESERVATIONS

First time Anchorage visitors are invariably surprised by the quality and breadth of Anchorage dining—the city is far smaller than other urban areas with comparable dining scenes. Some attribute that to the high volume of visitors and the long, dark winters during which a dinner out is a welcome treat; but it's just as accurate to say that Anchorage has a sense of pride in place that creates strong support for, among other things, a thriving restaurant scene. Several of the better-known downtown restaurants, such as Glacier Brewhouse and Orso, are vastly popular with tourists and thus very hard to get into mid-May through mid-September. Reservations are essential for dinner during the summer peak season—good advice for Fairbanks, Juneau and other major communities, especially cruise-ship ports of call.

Anchorage

Fire Island Rustic Bake Shop
$ Baked Goods
1343 G St. 907-569-0001.
www.fireislandbread.com.
No dinner. Closed Mon–Tue.
Sited in a small heritage house south of downtown, Anchorage's best artisan bakery specializes in handmade European-style pastries and breads—the latter of which are fashioned into hearty sandwiches. Croissants, muffins and scones comprise the morning fare. Each day's lunch offers three different sandwiches.

Lucky Wishbone
$ American
1033 E 5th Ave. 907-272-3454.
Closed Sun.
It may seem surprising to find a locally famous fried-chicken emporium in Anchorage—until you recall that a major military base, with service members from throughout America, sits just a

Coffee, Coffee Everywhere

Steamdot ©Steamdot

Anchorage, like Fairbanks, boasts an astounding affinity for coffee: coffee shops are ubiquitous, and drive-through espresso stands are even more so. City statistics show some 150 coffee shops and espresso stands in Anchorage, about one per 2,000 residents. The most prominent local purveyor is **Kaladi Brothers**, which roasts its own coffee and has a dozen outlets throughout south-central Alaska (*kaladi.com*). Newcomer **Steamdot Coffee** (*www.steamdot.com*), whose southside and downtown venues feature "coffee labs," offers customers a half-dozen different methods of coffee brewing, from classic espresso to a siphon brewer.

mile away. Lucky Wishbone serves up chicken pan-fried with a thin but crispy batter. The milkshakes are hugely popular too. Anchorage residents call this eatery just "the Bone."

Middle Way Café
$ American
1300 W Northern Lights Blvd.
907-272-6433. www.middleway
cafe.com. Breakfast and
Lunch only.

Located in a strip mall next to Anchorage's best and biggest bookstore, Middle Way offers simple fare finely prepared. Daily soups feature Alaska Grown ingredients; sandwiches use house-made bread.
Hot breakfasts mean pastries and the city's best French toast. Lunchtime is crowded with locals, but there is plenty of room.

Moose's Tooth Pub & Pizzeria

©Moose's Tooth Pub & Pizzeria

Moose's Tooth Pub & Pizzeria

$ Pizza

3300 Old Seward Hwy. 907-258-2537. www.moosestooth.net.
The lines are long at this astronomically popular midtown brewpub restaurant; the "Tooth" does not take reservations, and waits up to an hour are possible. The draw is pizza—most agree it's the best in Alaska, and certainly among the best in North America. Dozens of varieties include imaginative preparations such as chipotle steak and the "Avalanche," with pepperoni, blackened chicken, bacon, onions and three cheeses. Each month brings a different cheesecake to the dessert menu, such as blueberry in August.

Snow City Café

$ American

1034 W 4th Ave. 907-272-2489. www.snowcitycafe.com.
While it serves food throughout the day, breakfast is the draw here at the edge of downtown. The most famous item by far is the "Crabby" omelette, rich with snow crab and accompanied by superior hash browns made whenever possible using Alaska Grown potatoes. The eggs Benedict features salmon cakes, which can also be had with fired or scrambled eggs. The "Tundra Scramble" comes with reindeer sausage, mushrooms and onions. Long waits here are common on weekends and in summer.

Ginger

$$ Pacific Rim

425 W. 5th Ave. 907-929-3680. www.gingeralaska.com.
Though Asian influences are widespread at this downtown bistro, its menu is expansive enough to include Continental and Caribbean hints—jambalaya with shrimp, scallops, linguica sausage and peppers in a red sauce, for instance, or beef tips in coconut curry. This restaurant flies below the tourist radar, so tables are often available when other restaurants have lines going out the door.

Glacier Brewhouse

$$ Pub Food

737 W 5th Ave. 907-274-2739. www.glacierbrewhouse.com.
Reservations essential year-round.

Glacier Brewhouse

© Glacier Brewhouse

©Drew Johnson/Kincaid Grill

Kincaid Grill

This vast, always bustling downtown eatery is built on its brewpub foundation—eight brews are on tap at any given time— but goes far beyond that with expertly prepared savory food. A large rotisserie uses alder wood to smoke-roast chicken, beef and pork; salmon, halibut and cod are offered in intriguing presentations, such as halibut crusted with herbs and spent-grain breadcrumbs.

Kincaid Grill
$$ Regional Alaskan
6700 Jewel Lake Rd. 907-243-0507.
www.kincaidgrill.com.
Chef Al Levinsohn, a pioneer of Alaska Regional cuisine, offers gourmet fine dining in a rather unprepossessing strip mall in south Anchorage—a location that helps fend off tour-group crowds. The menu has Mediterranean hints: Kodiak scallops, for example, come with haricot vert and olive tapenade; king crab is the foundation of the bouillabaisse.

ORSO
$$ Mediterranean
737 W 5th Ave. 907-222-3232.
www.orsoalaska.com.
Mediterranean influences mark the menu at this vastly popular downtown dining room. The wide-ranging menu includes steaks and burgers, pastas and entrée salads; but the highlight is an expansive seafood menu of salmon, halibut, sole, rockfish, albacore, king crab and more—all Alaskan or Pacific in origin. The signature dish is wild salmon baked on cedar planks, reflecting the traditional Native coastal presentation.

ORSO
© ORSO

Simon & Seafort's
$$ **Seafood and Steaks**
420 L St. 907-274-3502.
www.simonandseaforts.com.
Seafood is the raison d'être for this downtown chophouse popular with business travelers.
The setting at the west end of downtown overlooks Cook Inlet and Mount Susitna in the distance. The dishes are mainstream—fish and chips, fish tacos, cioppino, steaks, steamed crab and clams, and applewood smoked meats—but they are expertly prepared. The signature starters are gin-cured salmon carpaccio and smoked salmon rangoons.

Southside Bistro
$$ **Regional Alaskan**
1320 Huffman Park Dr. 907-348-0088. www.southsidebistro.com.
Almost exclusively the province of Anchorage residents, this fine-dining establishment is housed in an undistinguished strip mall. The eclectic menu ranges from Scandinavian style duck to chile-rubbed skirt steak, but the highlight is the daily chalkboard menu of fresh seafood specials—such as halibut pan roasted with mushrooms and miso. The signature starter uses Kodiak scallops with risotto and truffled shellfish cream.

Marx Brothers Café
$$$ **Regional Alaskan**
627 W 3rd Ave. 907-278-2133.
www.marxcafe.com. Closed Sun and Mon.
This small fine-dining restaurant, housed in a heritage frame home overlooking Ship Creek, helped pioneer gourmet cuisine in Anchorage in the late 1970s as an outgrowth of a dinner club. The firelit atmosphere is quiet and convivial. The menu remains one of the most sophisticated in Alaska, with an emphasis on seafood: halibut macadamia, grilled salmon with peach butter, scallops and Pacific prawns with garlic stuffing. The classic Caesar salad is among the best anywhere.
The cafe also operates the **Muse** restaurant at the Anchorage Museum, which serves exceptional halibut burgers and sweet potato fries.

Seven Glaciers Restaurant
$$$ **Regional Alaskan**
Alyeska Resort, Girdwood. 907-754-2237. www.alyeskaresort.com.
Veteran Alaska diners often consider this Girdwood standout the Anchorage area's best restaurant. Its setting is superb—sitting at the upper terminal of the Alyeska Tram, overlooking Turnagain Arm and the Kenai Mountains. Its commitment to Alaskan foods is thorough: crab cakes and scallop bisque are the signature appetizers, and the menu occasionally features Alaska-raised elk or bison. Expert preparations of salmon and halibut top the regular dinner menu, and vegetarian and gluten-free menus are offered nightly. The memorable tram ride up and back is free for dinner guests.

Denali Park Area

229 Parks
$$ **Regional Alaskan**
MP 229 George Parks Hwy. 907-683-2567. 229parks.com. Dinner only (Sunday brunch in summer). Closed Mon.

Seven Glaciers Restaurant

© Ken Graham Photography

Housed in a charming log lodge a half-hour south of the Denali National Park entrance, this outpost of gourmet cuisine represents the best food between Anchorage and Fairbanks. Local art lines the walls, and chef-owner Laura Cole makes a point of relying on Interior Alaska food purveyors for delights such as potato-leek soup and regional seafood.

Fairbanks

Alaska Coffee Roasters

$ Baked Goods-
          Delicatessen
4001 Geist Rd. 907-457-5282.
www.alaskacoffeeroasting.com.
Fairbanks's home-grown coffee roaster is also a splendid bakery whose signature pizzas (called flatbreads here) are the best in town. The Salinas is topped with roasted red peppers, garlic and provolone; the Alsace has Black Forest ham and Emmenthaler. The Key lime pie is a huge favorite. For truly global travelers, there's also a location in Miami, Florida.

LuLu's Bakery

$ Baked Goods
275 Riverstone. 907-374-3804.
Breakfast and Lunch only.
Closed Mon.
Superb handmade breads and pastries constitute the fare at this cozy bakery near the university campus. Each day brings a different bread—walnut sourdough on Tuesday, for instance—and morning pastries include local fruit such as blueberries and raspberries when they're available. Sandwiches are on offer for both breakfast and lunch, made with LuLu's European-style loaves like whole wheat sourdough.

Silver Gulch Brewery

$ Pub Food
*2195 Old Steese Hwy. 907-452-
2739. www.silvergulch.com.*
"America's Most Northern Brewery," as this vast facility fashions itself, is north of Fairbanks in a historic mining district known as Fox. Aside from the brewery's products, the menu ranges broadly across burgers, pizzas, fish and chips and pasta dishes; one signature entrée is a blueberry-glazed pork chop.

MUST EAT

Desserts include bread pudding and chocolate cake using Silver Gulch stout ale.

🦀 Gambardella's
$$ **Italian**
706 Second Ave. 907-457-4992. www.gambardellas.com.
Long a favorite with locals, this Italian fine-dining standout occupies a stand-alone heritage building downtown. Eclectic decor favors a wine grape theme. The menu is devotedly Italian, with a famous 10-layer lasagna that includes house-made sausage; and a flank steak stuffed with prosciutto, sun-dried tomatoes, mozzarella, basil and spinach. Salmon makes an appearance in the blackened sockeye Caesar salad.

Lavelle's Bistro
$$ **Regional Alaskan**
575 First Ave. 907-450-0555. www.lavellesbistro.com.
Fairbanks's closest exemplar of an artisan chef-driven restaurant, this perennially packed downtown dining room is filled with mirrors and conversational buzz.

Potato-crusted salmon stars as the signature seafood dish; the very popular, redolent meatloaf packs more than two dozen ingredients. The lavish wine cellar is the most extensive in the Alaska Interior.

🦀 Pumphouse
$$ **Regional Alaskan**
796 Chena Pump Rd. 907-479-8452. www.pumphouse.com.The large tin building along the Chena River that houses this local favorite eatery was originally an industrial pumphouse providing pressurized water to Fairbanks placer mining operations—the light standards on the riverside deck are old hose nozzles. During good weather the deck is likely the most appealing dinner spot in town.
The menu ranges from the requisite salmon and crab to unique items such as reindeer tenderloin, a domestic caribou steak with memorably deep flavor. The signature starter is halibut cheek ceviche, an unusual take on a favorite Alaskan delicacy.

Pumphouse

© Alaska Stock/agefotostock

Salt

© Sydney Talbott/Salt

Juneau

Heritage Coffee
$ Baked Goods
174 S Franklin St. 907-586-1087.
www.heritagecoffee.com.
Alaska's original artisan coffee
roaster dates back to the 1970s.
Today its coffees are found
throughout Southeast Alaska.
The company's cafes offer fresh
baked goods and quiches, as
well as soups, salads and
sandwiches for lunch—all made
using artisan bread and local
ingredients where possible.
Other locations include 216 2nd
St.; in the Safeway shopping
center; and at the Mendenhall
Glacier Visitor Center.

Twisted Fish
$$ Seafood
550 S. Franklin St. 907-463-5033.
www.twistedfishcompany.com.
Open seasonally in summer,
this waterfront bistro is located
near the Mount Roberts Tram.
Large windows and a light-wood
decor give the popular seafood
restaurant an airy feel. The
extensive menu features many
preparations of salmon, halibut,

cod and black cod as well as other
fish. Burgers and pizzas round
out the fare. Outside dining offers
views of the Gastineau Channel
and the nearby cruise-ships docks.

The Rookery
$$$ Regional Alaskan
111 Seward St. 907-463-3013.
therookerycafe.com.
Twice nominated for a James
Beard award, innovative chef Beau
Schooler has both revolutionized
and significantly raised the bar in
Alaska cuisine. Confronted with
dishes such as sockeye salmon
poached in duck fat and scallop
ceviche served with squid ink
adobo, most connoisseurs believe
The Rookery's cuisine is the best in
the state.

Salt
$$$ Regional Alaskan
200 Seward St. 907-780-2221.
saltalaska.com.
This white-linen establishment
is Juneau's fine dining standout,
a place where the service,
atmosphere and food all reach
high levels. Diners enjoy the likes
of sensational calamari, hand-
made pasta, and Alaskan gumbo

MUST EAT

based on North Pacific ingredients. The wine list is appropriately comprehensive.

Taku Glacier Lodge
$$$$ **Seafood**
Taku Inlet (floatplane access from Juneau only). 907-586-6275. www.wingsairways.com.
A big portion of the appeal of this popular Juneau-area attraction is the scenic floatplane flight to and from the lodge. Once they arrive, guests experience a classic Alaskan lodge dinner: alder-wood-roasted fresh salmon, plus traditional accompaniments such as baked beans, sourdough bread, coleslaw and biscuits, all handmade. Glacier ice is used to chill drinks, carved from the lodge's namesake glacier across the inlet on which the planes land. The tour-and-dinner package costs $290.

Kodiak

Mill Bay Coffee
$ **Baked Goods**
3833 Rezanoff Dr. E. 907-486-4411. www.millbaycoffee.com. Breakfast and Lunch only.
Kodiak Island's homegrown coffee roaster also offers a dandy selection of baked goods, mostly of the breakfast persuasion—large and hearty muffins, scones, croissants and other morning goods suited to a cool, temperamental climate. Flat breads and sandwiches round out the lunch menu.

Old Powerhouse
$$ **Seafood**
516 Marine Way E. 907-481-1088.
This waterfront restaurant's home is indeed an old powerhouse beside the channel along downtown Kodiak, so the setting is invariably scenic, with boats of every type cruising by. Asian preparations dominate the menu, with sushi, sashimi and tempura based on local seafood, and salmon drizzled with miso butter. A signature novelty is the seaweed salad, which surprises first-timers with its savory crunch.

Sitka

Homeport Eatery
$ **American**
209 Lincoln St. 907-623-0850. Breakfast and Lunch only.
This welcoming cafe on downtown Sitka's main street offers expertly executed everyday food and coffee drinks, ranging from morning pastries to bountiful sandwiches and hearty soups. Particularly notable is the best gluten-free bread in Southeast Alaska, making this restaurant one of the few places gluten-intolerant travelers can have a good sandwich.

Ludvig's Bistro
$$ **Regional Alaskan**
256 Katlian St., 907-966-3663 www.ludvigsbistro.com. Opening times limited in winter; call ahead.
Founded by two Sitka residents who wanted to improve the quality of dining in the city, Ludvig's lends a distinctly Mediterranean slant to its largely seafood-weighted menu. Breads and desserts are all made in-house, and dinner standouts include paella using local fish and shellfish; a spicy Spanish-style clam chowder; and fish and chips made using rockfish, the local "snapper."

HOTELS

Alaska may be tailor-made for adventure seekers in the great outdoors, but the state also offers a variety of comfortable overnight accommodations for every wallet. Lodgings range from primitive campgrounds and homey bed-and-breakfast inns to remote wilderness lodges, and posh resorts incorporating every modern convenience. Find your place to bed down for the night, lulled by the howl of a wolf or the whistle of a train.

PRICES AND AMENITIES

The properties listed herein were selected for their ambience, location and/or value for money. Prices reflect the average cost for a standard **double room** for two people in high season, not including taxes or surcharges. The hotel pricing categories shown above correspond to peak summer travel in Alaska (May 20 through August 20). Independent travelers with the freedom to visit Alaska in the **shoulder season** or in winter can benefit from hotel discounts of 50 percent or more, except in business hotels in Anchorage, which is the state's business center. Because of the huge volume of tour-based travel in Alaska, independent travelers visiting in **peak season** must make reservations well before the trip, lest you wind up bed-less in Bettles, for example.

Luxury	$$$$$	over $350
Expensive	$$$$	$250 to $350
Moderate	$$$	$175 to $250
Inexpensive	$$	$100-175
Budget	$	less than $100

TYPES OF LODGINGS

Two **hotel chains** in the Great Land are, uniquely, owned and operated by the state's two largest cruise companies, Holland America and Princess. Both are utilized for several facets of cruise trips— hotels in Anchorage and Juneau house guests before and after cruises, while those in the rest of the state hold the many travelers who have added land-based journeys to their cruise.

Holland America's **Westmark Hotels** consist of properties in Anchorage, Juneau, Fairbanks, Sitka, Skagway and Tok in Alaska, and Beaver Creek, Dawson City and Whitehorse in the Yukon (*800-544-0970; www.westmarkhotels.com*).

Princess Lodges are found in Fairbanks; on the Kenai Peninsula at Cooper Landing; near Wrangell St. Elias National Park in Copper Creek; and in two locales near Denali National Park, at the Denali park entrance and south of the national park at Denali State Park (*800-425-0500; www.princesslodges.com*). Each chain offers good quality at its lodgings—in some locales the Westmark and Princess properties are among the top accommodations in town, such as Fairbanks and at Denali.

The hotels range in size from roughly 100 to more than 600 units; rooms are generally spacious, up-to-date, clean and comfortable. While the vast majority of summertime guests are on cruise tours, both chains welcome independent travelers. Most major lodging chains have

© Alaska Stock Images / age fotostock

Camping, Denali National Park

properties in Anchorage and, to a lesser extent, Fairbanks—Best Western, Sheraton, Hilton, Motel 6, Holiday Inn, Marriott and the like are all represented in Alaska, for those who prefer to stick to particular national brands. Chains are less well represented in outlying locations such as Sitka, Ketchikan and Seward. Visitor bureaus for all locales offer complete lodging information. **Bed-and-breakfast inns** are less numerous in Alaska than in other US states. The state's major B&B group, **Bed and Breakfast Association of Alaska**, lists about two dozen good quality small inns (*www.alaskabba.com*).

Camping in established **campgrounds** is available at many state parks and at Denali National Park, Wrangell St. Elias National Park, and at numerous locales within Chugach National Forest and Tongass National Forest. (The latter has several car-camping facilities near Alaska Marine Highway ferry terminals, plus numerous public-use cabins and boat-access wilderness campgrounds.) Fees, facilities, seasons and access vary widely; be sure to obtain exact information before scheduling a stop at a particular campground. Reservations are available at a few sites—and highly advisable at Denali National Park.

Information on camping throughout the state is available at the various **Public Lands Information Centers** in Fairbanks, Anchorage, Tok and Ketchikan (*www.alaskacenters.gov*). The *Milepost* annual guide to driving the Alaska Highway includes comprehensive information on both public and private campgrounds (*see Excursions, Fairbanks chapter*).

A small community of **wilderness lodges** provides accommodations and adventure to travelers seeking an experience in "the bush." One need not visit a wilderness lodge to see wildlife, go fishing, hunting, hiking or pursue other outdoor activities; but flying or boating in to a small lodge set on a remote lake, river or inlet somehow equates to a more serene, intense experience.

Lodges range from activity-oriented modern facilities to fishing cabins at which daylight

HOTELS

143

hours are devoted to being on the water. Comfort, amenities, food and ease of access vary widely; but getting to most of these lodges requires a **floatplane flight** to reach the lodge, and that expense figures significantly in the total cost. Some lodges focus heavily on gourmet Alaskan Regional cuisine, utilizing ingredients such as seafood and berries that guests might pick themselves.

Others are almost exclusively devoted to wildlife watching and have resident naturalist guides on hand to offer interpretation and answer guests' questions.

Some Alaska lodges with "wilderness" in their name are actually reached by road, but border wilderness areas.

Most such lodges operate only May through September. A complete inventory of the state's roughly 60 lodges is available on the official state travel website *www.travelalaska.com*.

For more about the wilderness lodging experience, see **Into the Wild** at the end of this chapter.

Touring Tip

Many properties offer special packages and weekend rates that may not be extended in peak summer months (*late May–late Aug*) and holiday seasons, especially near major destinations like Denali National Park. Advance reservations are recommended at all times. Rates are always higher from May 15 to September 15; and, in Anchorage in early March around Iditarod time.

Anchorage

Alaska Backpackers Inn
$ 24 rooms
409 Eagle St. 907-277-2770. alaskabackpackers.com.
Spread across several buildings on the east end of downtown, this hostel offers clean, quiet accommodations ranging from dorm rooms to family rooms with private baths. Laundry, Internet, storage and cooking facilities expand the hostel's utility for economy travelers.

Copper Whale Inn
$$ 14 rooms
440 L St. 907-258-7999 or 866-258-7999. www.copperwhale.com.
Perched atop the bluff at the west end of downtown, this small inn has spacious rooms done in coral and copper shades, with a small courtyard. Two rooms share a bath. Continental breakfasts come with expert advice from the innkeepers about nearby attractions, like the Tony Knowles Coastal Trail two blocks away (bike rentals on-site). The view of Cook Inlet from the breakfast lounge is superb.

Historic Anchorage Hotel
$$$ 26 rooms
330 E St. 907-272-4553 or 800-544-0988. www.historic anchoragehotel.com.
Downtown Anchorage's only historic hotel sits on the hill above Ship Creek; all of downtown's sights lie within easy walking distance. Established in 1916, when Anchorage was still largely a tent town, the hotel was restored in 1989 and features period furnishings such as brocade upholstery, patterned carpets

and Edwardian side tables. A fitness center, Internet service and complimentary newspaper complete the modern touches.

Inlet Tower Hotel
$$$ **180 rooms**
1200 L St. 907-276-0110 or 800-544-0786. www.inlettower.com.
Towering above a residential neighborhood along Chester Creek, this business-oriented hotel has large rooms and suites at relatively modest prices. Most of the rooms offer expansive views of Cook Inlet or the Chugach Mountains; the decor features warm rust and red tones with light wood furniture. Inlet Tower is very popular with Asian travelers here for Northern Lights viewing.

Hotel Alyeska
$$$$ **304 rooms**
1000 Arlberg Ave., Girdwood. 907-754-2111 or 800-880-3880. www.alyeskaresort.com.
Although the main lodge for the Alyeska Resort ski area looks like a massive block towering over the surrounding forest, it suits the scale of the mountain above it.

Rooms within are warm, quiet and spacious; they permit splendid mountain views no matter which way they face. The tram base sits at the foot of the hotel, so skiers walk only a few paces to hit the slopes.

Hotel Captain Cook
$$$$ **547 rooms**
939 W. 5th Ave. 907-276-6000 or 800-843-1950. captaincook.com.
The Captain Cook is generally considered Anchorage's best hotel. Its three copper-colored reflective towers occupy an entire block at the west end of downtown. Rooms are commodious, decorated in neutral beiges and greens; many on the north and west sides have views of Denali on clear days. The hotel's ample shops, meeting rooms and restaurants make it a top choice for business travelers. The **Crow's Nest ($$$)**, a fine dining restaurant atop the highest tower, has expansive views of the city and entire Cook Inlet region, all the way to Denali. Illustrating the exploits of Capt. Cook, lobby walls sport murals and maps.

Breakfast bar, Historic Anchorage Hotel

© Historic Anchorage Hotel

Hotel Alyeska with Northern Lights

© HagePhoto.com/Alyeska Resort

Lakefront Anchorage Hotel
$$$$ 248 rooms
*4800 Spenard Rd. 907-243-2300
or 866-866-8086.*
www.millenniumhotels.com.
Best known as the headquarters
hotel for the Iditarod start in
March, this hotel lies the closest to
Anchorage International Airport—
in fact, it's on an arm of Lake Hood,
the airport's floatplane base.
Guests can book a charter flight
that departs from the hotel's own
dock. Larger than hotel standard,
rooms are basic, done up with
green tones. Guests seeking quiet
will appreciate the surrounding
residential neighborhood.

Dalton Highway

Coldfoot Camp
$ 24 rooms
MP 175 Dalton Hwy. 907-474-3500.
coldfootcamp.com.
The only real stopping point on the
Dalton Highway is this uniquely
Alaska outpost 50mi north of the
Arctic Circle. It offers a parking
lot full of trucks and adventure
vehicles; a classic diner; and
lodging composed of Atco trailers,
the quintessential Arctic portable
housing. Accommodations are,
well, basic; but the place is like
nowhere else in the US.

Lakefront Anchorage Hotel

©Millennium Alaskan Hotel

Fairbanks

A Taste of Alaska Lodge
$$$ 10 rooms
551 Eberhardt Rd. 907-488-7855.
www.atasteofalaska.com.
Set astride a low ridge outside
Fairbanks proper, this rambling
complex has three personalities.
It is first of all a quasi-museum with
a collection of Alaskana few can
match—down to the mid-century
hand-soap dispensers in the lobby
restrooms. Posters, artifacts, books
and oddments abound, and it
would take hours just to view
them all. Secondly, it is a premier
spot for Northern Lights viewing
in winter—open meadows with
wide views of the sky lie below the
lodge on 280 acres of land, and the
city's lights do not intrude this far
out in the country. Lastly, its dining
room is a well-known practitioner
of Alaska Regional cuisine;
breakfasts focus on handmade
sourdough and reindeer sausage,
for instance. Rooms are cozy and
feature eclectic decor—but one
isn't here to spend much time in
the room. Unlike so many other
Alaska lodgings, its rates stay the
same year-round.

Pike's Waterfront Lodge
$$$ 208 rooms
1850 Hoselton Dr. 907-456-4500
or 877-774-2400.
www.pikeslodge.com.
This light-filled, warm and
welcoming wood lodge lies along
the Chena River, not far from the
airport. A full-fledged business
hotel as well as tourist lodging, it
has superbly comfortable rooms
in many configurations, from
standard to "royal rooms," all
with brocade bedspreads, neo-
Victorian furnishings and modern
amenities such as Wi-Fi throughout
the resort. Pike's is a leader in
sustainability and has replaced
plastics with compostables in its
cafe, donates its cooking oil to a
biofuels co-op, and avidly recycles
paper products.

River's Edge Resort
$$$ 94 rooms
4200 Boat St. 907-474-0286 or 800-
770-3343. www.riversedge.net.
This charming accommodation
consists largely of tidy, white-sided
cottages set along the Chena River
and beside gardens throughout
the grounds of the hotel. Huge
flower baskets decorate each cozy

A Taste of Alaska Lodge

© A Taste of Alaska Lodge

HOTELS

cottage. Inside, guest quarters are pleasant, done in farmstead style with flower bedspreads and sitting patios. Shuttle service to the airport, railroad station and nearby attractions is free.

Adjacent to the resort, 🍴 **Chena's Alaskan Grill ($$)** has a splendid deck overlooking the river, and a menu focusing on Alaska seafood.

Haines

Hotel Halsingland
$$ 35 rooms
13 Fort Seward Dr. 907-766-2000. hotelhalsingland.com.
This venerable historic property, comprising 1901 former officers' quarters, bestrides a hillside overlooking the town; its spacious rooms feature early 20C furnishings and old-growth fir trim. The on-site restaurant is the best in town, focusing on Southeast Alaska seafood.

Juneau Area

Alaska's Capital Inn
$$$ 7 rooms
113 W Fifth St. 907-588-6507 or 888-588-6507.
www.alaskacapitalinn.com.
Poised atop the hill overlooking downtown Juneau, this excellent small inn is popular with state officials when the Alaska Legislature is in session. The 1906 house is Edwardian in design, and both the public areas and the rooms themselves are discreetly furnished with period appointments such as potbelly stoves, pedestal beds, and handmade quilts. Lavish hot breakfasts feature rhubarb muffins, sourdough pancakes and thick-slab bacon. The State Capitol, Alaska State Museum and downtown waterfront are within easy walking distance.

Four Points Sheraton
$$$ 106 rooms
51 Egan Dr. 907-586-6900 or 888-478-6909.
www.goldbelthotel.com.
Completely renovated and improved, the former Goldbelt Hotel is now Juneau's best mainstream lodging. This seven-story accommodation sits just above the waterfront in the city's downtown, convenient to most sights in Juneau. Rooms

Gustavus Inn

are functional and clean, with varying bed combinations and room configurations. A free airport shuttle is a bonus for hotel guests. There's an on-site restaurant.

🛏 Gustavus Inn

$$$ (inclusive) 9 rooms
1 Gustavus Rd., Gustavus (Glacier Bay). 907-697-2254 or 800-649-5220. www.gustavusinn.com. Closed in winter.

Set bestride meadows with flowering borders and woods in the distance, this small inn topped by a red roof carries a Scandinavian aura unique in Alaska. A converted 1928 homestead, the inn features a hearth room and library in addition to its cozy, farmstead-style rooms (two with shared bath) appointed with flowered quilts and wicker furnishings. Meals (all are included in the rate) focus on local seafood. Shuttle service is available to and from the airport and elsewhere. The lodge arranges kayaking, flightseeing and fishing.

🛏 Pearson's Pond Luxury Inn

$$$$ 7 rooms
4541 Sawa Circle. 907-789-3772. pearsonspond.com.

There is indeed a pond on the wooded grounds of this deluxe small inn outside Juneau, but most guests are here not to meditate. They arrive to get married, celebrate anniversaries—or visit nearby Mendenhall Glacier. The inn's spacious rooms and suites are decorated in earth tones of forest green, warm wood, sand and sage. Hot tubs on the deck, a full-service spa, a fitness center and outdoor gear for rental buttress activities like glacier trekking.

Kennecott

Kennicott Glacier Lodge

$$ 44 rooms.
15 Kennicott Millsite. 907-258-2350. kennicottlodge.com.

This charming facility enjoys a site overlooking the old copper mine millworks, the area's two glaciers, and the peaks of Wrangell-St. Elias National Park. Its historic character belies its modern construction; rooms are spare but comfy, and the food is excellent. Access is by pre-arranged shuttle from the McCarthy Road.

Garden view, Pearson's Pond Luxury Inn

Courtesy of Pearson's Pond

HOTELS

149

Talkeetna Alaskan Lodge

© Frank Flavin photography/Alaska Collection

Kodiak

🏠 A Channel View B&B

$$ 4 rooms (2-night minimum).

1010 Stellar Way. 907-486-2470.
www.kodiakchannelview.com.
Owned and operated by a fifth-generation Alaskan who traces her ancestry back to the state's Russian colony days, this fine small inn perches on a bluff overlooking the channel east of the city center. It permits great views of the water, passing boats and wildlife. Two of the units are comfortably furnished, spacious apartment-suites, with sitting areas, kitchenettes, private baths and ample room to spread out.

Kodiak Hilltop B&B

$$ 5 rooms

993 Hilltop Dr. 907-486-4862.
www.kodiakhilltopbnb.com.
Located 4mi from town and across from a state park, this two-story house offers four basic ground-floor bedrooms with two shared baths and a two-bedroom suite upstairs with 1.5 bathrooms. Amenities include laundry facilities, lots of parking, Wi-Fi and a common kitchen.

Seward Area

🏠 Seward Windsong Lodge

$$$$ 180 rooms

Mile 0.5 Exit Glacier Rd.
907-224-7116 or 877-777-4079.
www.sewardwindsong.com.
Closed in winter.
Located just outside Seward, this large lodge is a center of Kenai Peninsula outdoor activities for travelers—hikes up to the glacier nearby, scenic cruises through Resurrection Bay, fishing in both salt and fresh water venues for salmon. Rooms are functional and newly remodeled. The lodge's restaurant, **Resurrection Roadhouse ($$$)**, is a leading practitioner of Alaskan Regional cuisine, with dishes such as 🍽 **bison burger**, semolina-crusted halibut, and salmon with potato confit.

Kenai Fjords Wilderness Lodge

$$$$$ 8 rooms

Fox Island (boat access only)
877-777-4053. www.kenaifjords
lodge.com. Closed in winter.
Only boats (and the occasional floatplane) access this remote lodge about 10mi south of Seward in Resurrection Bay. Guests stay

MUST STAY

in newly refurbished cabins with sitting areas, private baths and porches overlooking the water and Kenai Mountains beyond. Prices include boat transport and all meals.

Sitka

Otter's Cove B&B
$$$ 3 rooms
3211 Halibut Point Rd. 907-747-4529. www.ottercovebandb.com.
Overlooking Sitka Sound from its waterfront location 3mi north of Sitka's city center, this fine bed and breakfast inn has three spacious rooms with views of the Sound and all that ply the rich waters—sea otters, humpback whales, bald eagles, dolphins and other marine life. The simply furnished rooms are done in light colors; two of the rooms have extra bed space to house families. The outside hot tub provides a splendid vantagepoint to see Sitka Sound.

Shee Atika Totem Square Inn
$$$ 68 rooms
201 Katlian St. 907-747-3693 or 866-300-1353.
totemsquarehotelmarina.com.
Situated right on the waterfront downtown, this fine business hotel is owned and operated by the local Native corporation. Sitka sights, including the National Historical Park, are within easy walking distance. The recently remodeled rooms are clean and well-kept. Full business services include Wi-Fi throughout, a business center, fitness center and airport shuttle service. The on-site **Dock Shack Café ($$)** serves expert preparations of local seafood.

Talkeetna

Talkeetna Roadhouse
$ 12 rooms
Main St at C St. 907-733-1351.
www.talkeetnaroadhouse.com.
Talkeetna's famous facility consists of a historic roadhouse containing various rooms with shared bath, cabins out back, and a pioneer cabin down the road a bit, with no indoor toilet. The roadhouse serves as an inn, a restaurant and a community gathering point. That's what roadhouses used to be, and what this one was when it opened around 1917. The historic character is conspicuous: tilting floors, dark log walls, low ceilings. As this is a gathering spot for adventurers of all sorts, the atmosphere is convivial. The bakery's cinnamon rolls are known throughout south-central Alaska.

🛁 Talkeetna Alaskan Lodge
$$$$ 212 rooms
23601 Talkeetna Spur Rd.
907-733-9500 or 877-777-4067.
www.talkeetnalodge.com.
Closed in winter.
Sited atop a low bluff above Talkeetna proper, this handsome wood and stone lodge enjoys spectacular views of Denali, when the weather is clear. The cottonwood-lined Susitna River occupies the near foreground, making the lodge's long veranda a divine place to sit an hour and marvel at the beauty of Alaska. The lodge's six types of rooms provide great variety, from compact, functional hotel rooms to spacious suites with sitting rooms and views of Denali. Decor blends ivory and sand colors with red or blue accents.

INTO THE WILD

The vast majority of Alaska's territory is undeveloped wilderness—untracked mountains, forests, rivers and lakes that are the province of bears, caribou, moose, eagles, wolves and everything wild. No roads reach these places; few people live in the "bush." But that doesn't mean the Alaska traveler cannot visit it.

Wilderness lodges abound in the Great Land. They offer adventurous travelers the opportunity to engage in **activities** that make memorable experiences. Fishing, wildlife viewing, canoeing, kayaking, berry-picking, hiking and sightseeing can be within steps of your accommodation, and far from the crowds that populate the state's well-known destinations. Best of all, many lodges are quite **luxurious**, with upscale, cozy quarters in cabins or log lodges; there's no "roughing it" here. All must be reached by boat or floatplane, a journey that is, in itself, an adventure—and a great start to your wilderness stay; a booking almost always includes transportation arrangements. Accomplished chefs bring to table **gourmet meals** featuring local ingredients; trained guides help travelers aim their fly-fishing lines, watch wild bears in safety, and understand the complex environment that supports it all. Days of active outdoor adventure and sumptuous lodge meals are followed by a quick walk to your cabin for peaceful slumber with starlight brushing the windowsill. While the state's wilderness lodge industry dates back several decades, until recently the major focus was **fishing**—a fine outdoor thrill still available at virtually all such lodges. Many lodges are still devoted primarily to fishing, but the focus has broadened considerably in recent years. Nowadays travelers can have **options** like wellness retreats, yoga workshops, culinary lessons, photography courses, sketching and journaling, and all manner of other modern pursuits, way out in the wilds of Alaska. Though wilderness lodge stays

Moose in the bushes

Kayaking: a popular wilderness lodge activity

©Leslie Forsberg/Michelin

are **expensive**, prices include all activities and meals, along with (usually) transport to and fro. The official **Alaska travel website** has a section about wilderness lodges (*www.travelalaska.com*). Note that many lodges in Alaska with "wilderness" in their name are actually reached by road—but they do indeed have wilderness out their back door. Here are a few of our favorite lodges.

Within the Wild

This dynamic company operates two remote lodges in **south-central Alaska**. Both of them are upscale facilities overlooking lakes or bays. Comfortable deluxe cabins and lodge suites are well-appointed and spacious, complete with amenities such as woodstoves and sleeping lofts. **Tutka Bay Lodge** is the summer home of Chef Kirsten Dixon, one of the leaders of the Alaska Regional cuisine movement; her menus range widely from artisan cheese flown in weekly to salmon, halibut and lingcod caught nearby. Dixon's cuisine guides the menu at the

other lodge, **Winterlake** (**$$$$$**; *withinthewild.com*).

Kachemak Bay Wilderness Lodge

Located across the bay from Homer, this oceanfront facility provides accommodation in cozy cedar-shake cabins, with a main lodge, hot tub, sauna and solarium offering comfort in the wilderness. Tidepool explorations, fishing, kayaking, and wildlife watching are supplemented by top-notch cuisine focusing on local seafood (**$$$$**; *alaskawildernesslodge.com*).

Kenai Fjords Glacier Lodge

The only lodging inside Kenai Fjords National Park, this 16-cabin facility is situated on a flat bench of land across a large lagoon from Pederson Glacier. Kayaking, hiking and wildlife watching occupy time for guests, who arrive by boat from Seward; the same company operates two other lodges in the Kenai Peninsula interior, Kenai Backcountry and Kenai Riverside (**$$$$**; *kenaifjordsglacierlodge.com*).

ALASKA

W

Map Index